D0479811

NO LONGER PROPERTY OF
ANYTHINK LIBRARIES/
RANGEVIEW LIBRARY DISTRICT

# Designer
# Plant
# Combinations

# Designer Plant Combinations

## 105 Stunning Gardens Using Six Plants or Fewer

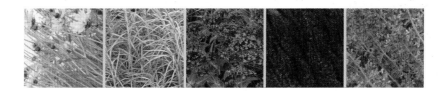

SCOTT CALHOUN

Storey Publishing

The mission of Storey Publishing is to serve our customers by
publishing practical information that encourages
personal independence in harmony with the environment.

Edited by Carleen Madigan Perkins
Art direction and book design by Mary Winkelman Velgos

Front cover photography by © Scott Calhoun: columns 1 top, 2, 3, 5, 7 and © Charles Mann: columns 1 middle,
     bottom, 4, 6
Back cover photography by © Charles Mann, except author photo by © Edward McCain
Interior photography by © Scott Calhoun, except for © Marion Brenner: 74–75; © Karen Bussolini: 130–131,
     137, 166–167, 180–181, 184–185; © Rob Cardillo: 6, 30–31, 65, 199, 214–215, 220–221; © Saxon Holt:
     118–119, 152-153, 210–211, 224–225; © Charles Mann: 2–3, 9, 10, 13, 18-19, 20–21, 22–23, 26-27, 34-35,
     44–45, 48–49, 50, 62–63, 78–79, 86–87, 91, 107, 128–129, 132–133, 177, 190–191; © Carrie Nimmer,
     Landscape Designer: 165, 172–173

Indexed by Christine Lindemer, Boston Road Communications

Text © 2008 by Scott Calhoun

All rights reserved. No part of this book may be reproduced without written permission from the publisher, except by a
reviewer who may quote brief passages or reproduce illustrations in a review with appropriate credits; nor may any part of this
book be reproduced, stored in a retrieval system, or transmitted in any form or by any means — electronic, mechanical, photo-
copying, recording, or other — without written permission from the publisher.
     The information in this book is true and complete to the best of our knowledge. All recommendations are made with-
out guarantee on the part of the author or Storey Publishing. The author and publisher disclaim any liability in connection
with the use of this information. For additional information, please contact Storey Publishing, 210 MASS MoCA Way, North
Adams, MA 01247.
     Storey books are available for special premium and promotional uses and for customized editions. For further information,
please call 1-800-793-9396.

Printed in China by R.R. Donnelley
10  9  8  7  6  5  4  3  2  1

Library of Congress Cataloging-in-Publication Data

Calhoun, Scott.
  Designer plant combinations / by Scott Calhoun.
     p. cm.
  Includes index.
  ISBN 978-1-60342-077-8 (pbk. : alk. paper)
  1. Gardening—United States.
  2. Gardens—United States—Design.
  3. Plants, Ornamental—Selection—United States.  I. Title.
SB451.3.C35 2008
712'.60973—dc22
                         2008022439

*People sometimes think that gardening and plants are somehow trivial pursuits, mere pastimes, hobbies, somehow irrelevant. Nothing could be further from the truth. Gardening is the most powerful sacrament that links mankind to the natural world. Only twelve thousand years ago humanity began to grow plants deliberately. Those first acts of gardening catapulted a million years' worth of hunting-gathering into the vertiginous explosion of higher civilization. Each time you put a trowel in the fragrant earth, you recapitulate that bold and terrible act.*

— Panayoti Kelaidis

## Acknowledgments

My most sincere thanks go out to the following, who graciously shared their time, gardens, and insights with me: Dan Benarcik at Chanticleer; Duncan Brine; Dave Buchanan; Karen Bussolini; Gloria Ciaccio at Chicago Botanic Garden; Stephanie Cohen; David Cristiani; Sharon Cybart at Olbrich Gardens; Neil Diboll; Janet Draper at the Smithsonian; Noel Gieleghem; Mary Lou Gross; Panayoti Kelaidis; Greg Foreman; Inta Krombolz; Longwood Gardens staff; Lynden B. Miller; Carrie Nimmer; Nancy Ondra; Piet Ouldolf; Judith Phillips; Scott Rothenberger; David Salman; Julie Siegel; Scott Spencer; Nan Sterman; Bill Thomas at Chanticleer; Marcia Tatroe; Brandon Tyson; Laurel Voran at Chanticleer; Lenny Wilson at Delaware Center for Horticulture; Jonathan Wright at Chanticleer.

Following spread: The drumstick flower heads of 'Purple Sensation' ornamental onion (*Allium aflatuense* 'Purple Sensation') stand at attention above the maroon leaves of 'Husker Red' penstemon (*Penstemon digitalis* 'Husker Red') in this planting at Chanticleer.

# INTRODUCTION

There has been a lot of talk about new trends in American gardening over the past few years, very little of which has had to do with plants. If you've spent any time at all surfing the yard-makeover shows on cable television, you might have noticed that plants are often talked about as stage props and window dressing for a patio, spa, or deck. The conventional wisdom suggests that with shrinking lot sizes and growing decks and patios, plants are on their way to being elbowed out of the garden by outdoor living spaces. As Piet Oudolf and Noel Kingsbury point out in their book, *Planting Design*, "garden design has become too much like interior design applied to the out-of-doors, with a focus on overnight transformation rather than the craft of growing and nurturing plants." This sort of "put them behind the Jacuzzi" mentality about plants got me wondering exactly how much plants — or rather the thoughtful arrangement of plants in gardens — matter anymore.

In my own garden design practice, I believe that plants matter a lot. I got into this business to work with roots and shoots rather than simply promoting the masonry trade. When I started this book, I suspected that other garden designers felt the same way. To find out, I traveled across the country photographing the work of designers and horticulturists and tapped a vein of plant passion that far exceeded my expectations. It turns out that plants *do* still matter, maybe more than ever. They are the raw material for the artists we call landscape designers.

The diversity of the plant combinations I found was endless — and the creativity of my fellow designers and horticulturists energized my hunt. I found designers using plants like painters and sculptors, shoehorning amazing collections into small urban lots, and bringing prairie plantings to the suburbs with gusto. Native plants were making their way into sophisticated city settings. I saw color put to fearless use — a monochromatic garden of gold and yellow plants and a scene of spiky succulents profiled against a pomegranate-colored wall. In choosing these garden vignettes, I focused on innovative ensembles with a sense of intention and purpose that could be called the "designer touch."

On the nursery side of things, these designers seemed to be working with improved and fortified plant palettes. New plants coming out of programs like Plant Select in Colorado were providing a steady supply of spectacular and especially tough cultivars to arid western states. Back East,

A vivid perennial trio of hummingbird mint (*Agastache cana*), Russian sage (*Perovskia atriplicifolia*), and 'Moonshine' yarrow (*Achillea* 'Moonshine') form a tough and colorful combination.

the National Wildlife Federation teamed with nurseries to grow and market a line of native plants called American Beauties, aimed at reacquainting people with the charms of our indigenous flora and its benefits for wildlife. All of these new plants seemed to bode well for anyone considering designing a garden around plants (as if a garden design could be based on anything else). In some of the combinations featured, the plants do a good amount of heavy lifting, sometimes eliminating the need for some of the expensive aforementioned outdoor living masonry.

As I visited gardens and took pictures for this book, it occurred to me that good plant combinations are a little like the stanzas of a poem. That is, like the stanza, they are not trying to be a whole garden but a self-contained little part of one. Each combination spotlights just a handful of plants and is a part of a garden that extends well beyond the frame of the photograph. We find ourselves wondering about the part of the garden out of the frame, and it is a pleasant mystery. I can assure you, there are compost piles and sheds and playhouses outside the frame, but within the bounds of my viewfinder, I found these nearly perfect vignettes.

There is the danger that as the writer of this sort of book, I will explain too much, and therefore diminish some of the tang, liberty, and force (to paraphrase Stanley Kunitz) of these artful plantings. My hope is that through words and pictures, I can tell you a bit about the plants, creativity, and places where these photos were taken, in a way that is useful but not too pedestrian. I hope that some of these plant portraits and stories will capture your imagination. Perhaps they will even inspire you to embellish or reinvent your own garden so that it too tells a new and beguiling tale.

Having said all that, one of the main goals of this book is to simplify and demystify some of the planting design process by breaking it into comprehensible chunks of two to six plants. These chunks, while not a substitute for a full-blown garden design, are a way to start using plants in your garden in an inventive fashion. Even the most jaded gardener can't help but raise an eyebrow at all the unexpected and astonishing ways that these designers and horticulturists use plants. I hope reading about these plant arrangements gets your creative juices flowing and drives you out into the garden, to surround yourself with new roots and shoots in a brand-new bed of your own conception, inspired by a design you read about here.

— *Scott Calhoun*

Sometimes two plants are all you need — in this case, white-flowered colewort (*Crambe cordifolia*) and Jupiter's beard (*Centranthus ruber*).

# PERENNIAL Partners

Perennials, plants whose life cycle extends over more than one growing season (and very often over many growing seasons), represent a sort of sophistication and durability that cannot be provided by annual bedding plants alone.

Traditionally, perennials are arranged meticulously by height and color. In fact, organizing by color is given a great amount of importance in a traditional perennial border. I'm happy to say that the rigidity of this style has been adapted and thoroughly deconstructed by contemporary designers and horticulturists.

So all of this begs the question: what do the designers in this book do differently with perennials? The answer is hard to generalize; yet there are some unmistakable trends.

The designers here traditionally like to break up the monotony of a bed of perennials planted in graduated heights (small to large) by throwing in bold sculptural plants and planting some tall plants in the front of the border; they value texture and shape more than flower color; they include a few, or a lot of, native plants; they rarely use only perennials, almost always mixing in woody trees and shrubs, annuals (including annual wildflowers), accent plants, and especially grasses. Many designers are adopting a more relaxed attitude toward perennial maintenance, which recognizes seedheads for their intrinsic beauty (especially in winter), form, and value as wildlife forage. This style puts off deadheading to allow longer appreciation of plant skeletons.

For you, the home gardener, this means that some old rules about garden design no longer apply; you have broad freedom to combine perennials with shrubs, accents, and grasses in whatever ways you find pleasing. If you want to let your seadheads mature to a russet brown before deadheading, you're free to do so, and you may even be considered avant-garde for your delayed efforts. Just the vast variety of perennial plants available might intrigue you, and hopefully the portraits here will get you started down an adventurous road in a well-heeled pair of garden clogs.

Drought-tolerant native perennials like orange globe mallow (*Sphaeralcea ambigua*) and broom dalea (*Dalea scoparius*) provide wildlife habitat in the garden.

# THE SUPERMODEL OF VERBENAS

The simple common name *tall verbena* doesn't really do justice to the chic looks of this slender, purple-blue, upright grower. I prefer to call it "the supermodel of verbenas." In this colorful assemblage, Olbrich Botanical Gardens' director of horticulture, Jeff Epping, pairs the skinny verbena with the native narrow-leaf blue star for an effect that is almost magical. The svelte stems of the verbena, usually a more diaphanous presence in the garden, really pop next to the fine-leaved, chartreuse mounds of narrow-leaf blue star. To complete the backdrop, Epping groups two sturdy ornamental grasses, one of medium height and one tall, along with a 'Royal Purple' smoke tree for a burgundy brushstroke.

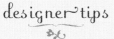

## designer tips

### Grow a Ball-Shaped Garden

There's nothing like a bunch of ball-shaped flowers on slender bloom stalks to make garden visitors stop and say, "Whoa!" or "Dude, where'd you get all these balls?" Clustering plants in the ornamental onion family (*Allium* spp.) with other spherical and hemispherical flowers in a single bed makes quite a design statement. In addition to the verbena featured here, experiment with star of Persia (*Allium christophii*), 'Summer Beauty' ornamental chives (*Allium tanguticum* 'Summer Beauty'), rattlesnake master (*Eryngium yuccifolium*), globe thistle (*Echinops ritro*), and 'Buddy' globe amaranth (*Gomphrena globosa* 'Buddy').

*Pair the skinny verbena with the native narrow-leaf blue star.*

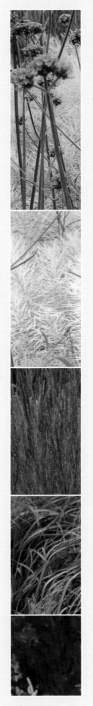

**Tall verbena**
*Verbena bonariensis*
This super-tall verbena grows up to five feet high with an open and airy habit that sways in the wind. A key attribute of this verbena is a transparency that allows it to be planted near the front of garden beds without obscuring plants behind it. Although it's treated as an annual in colder climates, it self-sows and comes back easily each year. Stray seedlings are relatively easy to thin out (but really, don't you want it everywhere?). Use it in combination with summer colors in the garden. As depicted here, tall verbena looks stunning when planted into a single-color mass of plants. Grow in moist but well-drained, moderately fertile soil in full sun. Hardy to Zone 7; used as a self-sowing annual elsewhere. 2'–4' tall × 18" wide.

**Narrow-leaf blue star**
*Amsonia hubrechtii*
This tall-grass prairie plant from Arkansas has made a big chartreuse splash in the garden world. As featured here at Olbrich Botanical Gardens in Madison, Wisconsin, it is well situated and color coordinated with tall verbena. Narrow-leaf blue star likes full sun and is tolerant of many soils, including clay. Clusters of steel-blue flowers appear in May and June. In fall, the fine needlelike leaves turn golden yellow. Hardy to Zone 4. 18"–24" tall × 18"–24" wide.

**'Avalanche' feather reed grass**
*Calamagrostis × acutiflora* 'Avalanche'
Used here as an intermediate grower behind the narrow-leaf blue star, 'Avalanche' is a variegated relative of the well-known 'Karl Foerster' feather reed grass. 'Avalanche' stands out for its lighter color (almost blue-gray here), which works nicely with the blue star. Likes full sun and moist, rich soils, including clay. Hardy to Zone 5. 3'–5' tall × 1'–2' wide.

**'Andante' maiden grass**
*Miscanthus sinensis* 'Andante'
This granddaddy of a grass forms a wall of green at the rear of the combination. The green leaves have a nice weeping habit and the grass flowers in generous plumes from late summer through fall. Reported not to produce seedlings, as many other maiden grasses do. Hardy to Zone 5. 7' tall × 2'–4' wide.

**'Royal Purple' smoke tree**
*Cotinus coggygria* 'Royal Purple'
The oval leaves are red-purple turning to scarlet in autumn. The plumelike panicles, which produce a summer display like puffs of smoke, give the plant its common name. Hardy to Zone 5. 15' tall × 15' wide.

15

# Dry-Garden Harmony

Although the blue, yellow, and purple sparkle, it's the different plant shapes that really make this combination stand. The pendulous clematis, umbel-form yarrow, and spherical star of Persia team up like a soprano, tenor, and baritone in a miniature choir of dry-garden plants. 'PS Harlan' hits the high notes, with 'Maynard's Gold' singing tenor and the star of Persia at the low end of the register. Greg Foreman, the designer of the combo, remarks that this arrangement is "all about form and texture; learning to mix pendulous flowers (clematis) with silver, fuzzy, hairy foliage (yarrow) and upright, globular blooms (allium)." This planting, by design, comprises only xeriscape (drought-tolerant) plants.

## designer tips

## When Things Get Hairy, Get Hairy Plants

*Hirsute, fuzzy, woolly, pubescent,* and *fringed* are all terms that describe plants with small hairs on their leaves and stems. Although hairiness is usually not an attribute that garden designers pay much attention to, fuzzy plants can be an asset when designing a garden. First off, the hairs on plants are often there to reflect sunlight and reduce water loss through the leaves. For this reason, hairy plants are almost always heat and drought tolerant. Hirsute plants are also more aesthetically pleasing than they are given credit for. Because the little hairs on plants catch light, they tend to be illuminated in the morning and evening hours, when the light is at a low angle, creating a glowing, three-dimensional look.

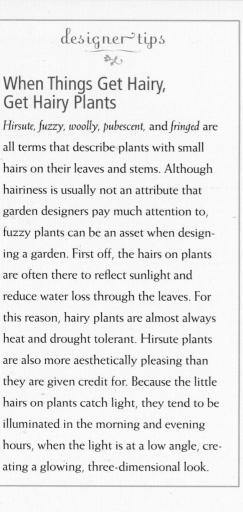

### 'PS Harlan' bush clematis
*Clematis integrifolia* 'PS Harlan'
Perhaps the most graceful of all the clematis, 'PS Harlan' is not really a twining plant but rather behaves more like an herbaceous perennial. Its remarkable two-inch pendulous flowers are periwinkle blue and are especially breathtaking, as illustrated here, when backlighting illuminates the silvery hairs along its stems and leaf margins. Provide sharp drainage and full sun. Hardy to Zone 4. 24" tall × 24" wide.

### 'Maynard's Gold' yarrow
*Achillea tomentosa* 'Maynard's Gold'
Intensely silver, woolly leaves and an unusually low profile for a yarrow make 'Maynard's Gold' a fine selection here. Unlike some yarrows, which would overwhelm surrounding plants, 'Maynard's Gold' is a compact ground-cover type. Its saturated yellow blooms are the perfect complement to 'PS Harlan' clematis. Hardy to Zone 3. 6" tall × 12" wide.

### Star of Persia
*Allium christophii* (*A. albopilosum*)
The eight-inch, metallic purple, spherical flower heads of star of Persia add a magical glow. Star of Persia is a bulb from Turkey with basal foliage (straplike leaves around the base of the plant) that blooms its huge, spherical flowers (shaped like drumsticks on steroids) in early summer. After the flower heads go to seed, the dried, globe-shaped heads are excellent in flower arrangements. Hardy to Zone 5. 12"–24" tall × 8"–12" wide.

### Alpine skullcap
*Scutellaria alpina*
Just creeping into the combination is the low mint-family plant skullcap, whose erect, purple, snapdragon-like flowers are reminiscent of penstemon. Hardy to Zone 5. 6"–10" tall × 12" wide.

Durable and elegant, this team of firewheel (*Gaillardia aristata)*, catmint (*Nepeta × faassenii)*, and 'Stella de Oro' daylily (*Hemerocallis* 'Stella de Oro') is well executed at the Yampa River Botanic Garden in Steamboat Springs, Colorado.

# Hummingbird Central

Like a flash of a rosy slip beneath a conservative, silver brocade dress, there's something a little exciting about finding orange and pink among such otherwise reserved silver plants. The pink rays and orange eye of 'Magnus' prairie coneflower provide the color template for this seductive combination put together by Santa Fe plantsman David Salman. He repeats the colors of the coneflower with 'Shades of Orange' hummingbird mint, grass-leaf red-hot poker, 'Powis Castle' artemisia, and woolly ironweed. In addition to being unusual in color, these are all drought-tolerant selections (as are most of David Salman's plant choices). The hot colors also attract more than the human eye, and both the red-hot poker and hummingbird mint are tailor-made for hummingbird beaks.

## designer tips

# Growing Hummingbird Mints

David Salman suggests growing hummingbird mints in areas where you can grow penstemons (*Penstemon*) and lavender (*Lavandula*) successfully. They like infertile, well-drained soils, prefer gravel mulches, and appreciate deep, infrequent watering. The most heat- and drought-tolerant *Agastache* species, *A. rupestris* (also known as licorice mint), is great for western climates with hot, sunny sites. If you garden in wetter eastern zones, consider Texas hummingbird mint (*Agastache cana*), 'Blue Fortune' hyssop (*Agastache* × 'Blue Fortune'), or 'Shades of Orange'; these three are better suited to average garden soil, increased humidity, and watering frequency.

*Set neon-colored flowers against silver foliage.*

### 'Shades of Orange' hummingbird mint
*Agastache aurantiaca* 'Shades of Orange'

The star of this combination, the flower spikes of 'Shades of Orange' range from tangerine to pink to red, successfully reflecting the colors of the adjacent prairie coneflower and providing a tall hummingbird magnet in the center of the combination. 'Shades of Orange' likes good garden soil. It's as much at home in the Mid-Atlantic as it is in the Southwest. Hardy to Zone 6 when planted in spring. (Agastaches and other heat-loving plants need a full season of warmth to establish good roots before winter.) 36" tall × 18" wide.

### 'Magnus' prairie coneflower
*Echinacea purpurea* 'Magnus'

Bolder flowers and deep green leaves bring prairie coneflower to the forefront of this combination. The pink and orange flowers of this tap-rooted prairie plant are the inspiration for this planting. The selection 'Magnus', the 1998 Perennial Plant of the Year, has huge flowers with petals that radiate out flat from the cone. Hardy to Zone 4. 36" tall × 18" wide.

### Grass-leaf red-hot poker
*Kniphofia triangularis* var. *triangularis*

The neon orange towers of grass-leaf red-hot poker act like exclamation points driving home the point that "we are orange and we grow upright!" Provide full sun and well-drained soil. Hardy to Zone 6. 24" tall × 18" wide.

### 'Powis Castle' artemisia
*Artemisia* × 'Powis Castle'

Although 'Powis Castle' is common in gardens in the Northeast, this tidy, mounding, silver-gray sage is one of the more underused sages — for no good reason — in southwestern gardens. Because it hardly ever flowers, 'Powis Castle' maintains its rounded appearance without deadheading, serving as a mounding foil to the otherwise vertical plants in this combination. It is drought tolerant and not fussy about soil types. Hardy to Zone 4. 36" tall × 30" wide.

### Woolly ironweed
*Vernonia lindheimeri* var. *incana*

Gardeners who know New York ironweed (*Vernonia noveboracensis*) might find woolly ironweed vaguely familiar, except for its foliage color, which is sterling silver — so silver, in fact, that it makes the other so-called silver plants look like dirty dish rags. This tall, steely plant, which was discovered in West Texas by the noted plantsman Scott Ogden, is the perfect backdrop for grass-leaf red-hot poker. In late September through October, woolly ironweed's tips explode with tiny, purple, daisylike flowers. It appreciates well-drained soil and is hardy to Zone 7. 3' tall × 18" wide.

# ALONG A POMEGRANATE WALL

Responding to a client who loved Spain and owned an Andalusian-style adobe home, landscape designer Carrie Nimmer began this project by proposing a fortress-thick garden wall to match the masculine nature of the house. After the wall was constructed, she painted it pomegranate red with a wink to Granada. The bold wall called for a bold planting, and Nimmer didn't hold back. Her daring plant program included two vivid desert wildflowers and twin-flowered agave. This highly saturated combo is able to withstand the intensity of the desert sun without washing out. Because the plants have silver and blue foliage and coral and yellow flowers, they play off the wall in dramatic fashion.

*Use bright wall colors as a backdrop for bold plantings.*

**Superb penstemon**
*Penstemon superbus*
The tubular, coral flowers of this showy, architectural specimen are a hummingbird favorite. Although the rosette of the plant is rather small, the bloom stalks can reach six feet tall if the conditions are right. Plant in well-drained soil and in full sun. It self-sows readily. Hardy to Zone 5. 2' tall × 2' wide.

**Sweet alyssum**
*Lobularia maritima*
Quick, fragrant, and dependable, sweet alyssum is a low grow-ing Mediterranean native. In cold-winter climes, sweet alyssum is grown as an annual spring through fall; in milder climates, it will bloom almost year round from seedlings. It is one of the few annual bedding plants tough enough to slug it out with native wildflowers and succulents. To keep sweet alyssum tidy, shear it back by half 4 weeks after its first bloom. Annual. 2"–12" tall × 12" wide.

**Twin-flowered agave**
*Agave geminiflora*
Normally a deep green, this twin-flowered agave has taken on a yellow hue. One of the switch hitters of the agave world, twin-flowered agave thrives in both sun and shade. In full sun, its tubular, straw-shaped leaves are still and upright; in shade, they relax and curve downward. Hardy to Zone 8. 3' tall × 3' wide.

**Desert marigold**
*Baileya multiradiata*
As likely to be found in a crack in the asphalt as in a garden, des-ert marigold is tough to beat for a super heat-tolerant perennial. Its intense yellow daisy flowers are displayed on slender, silver stems that rise from a tuft of silver foliage at the plant's base. It requires good drainage to succeed, and although it is short-lived, it self-sows readily. Hardy to Zone 6. 1' tall × 1' wide.

## *designer tips*

## Step Away from the Weeding Tools

One sure way to let naturalism creep into your garden is to relinquish a little control. Carrie Nimmer suggests letting a few plants, like superb penstemon and desert marigold, go to seed. "When you let your plants seed themselves, they find where they want to be, and the illusion of control slips away."

# Boss of Butterflies, Master of Rattlesnakes

Two upstanding, native prairie plants form the spine of this combination: ghostly white rattlesnake master and rosy pink common milkweed. Favorites of designer Julie Siegel, they give the arrangement a prairie context and proclaim, "This ecosystem is ours!" The common milkweed is a good plant for attracting monarch butterflies, but don't worry — the rattlesnake master doesn't attract rattlesnakes. Rather, it has roots that were used by Native Americans to concoct an antivenin for snakebites. In a garden, rattlesnake master's stiff stalks rise from yuccalike foliage, making it a natural centerpiece. Civilizing the natives, Siegel adds 'Summer Beauty' ornamental chive and behind that, a haze of blue Russian sage. This bed, surrounded by hot pavement, is a concrete example of how natives and exotics can be interspersed to excellent effect.

*Tough prairie natives and exotics fight it out in harsh, full-sun beds with little coddling.*

### Rattlesnake master

*Eryngium yuccifolium*

This member of the parsley family has pale, greenish white flowers that resemble spiky golf balls. True to its name, its spiky rosette of waxy, gray foliage looks similar to that of yuccas. Its common name is derived from its use by Native Americans as a snakebite remedy. In gardens it is excellent as a specimen, planted in threes, or even en masse. Zone 4. 3'–5' tall × 12" wide.

### 'Summer Beauty' ornamental chives

*Allium tanguticum 'Summer Beauty'*

The deep green, shiny leaves of 'Summer Beauty' are graced with two-foot-tall, pink pom-pom flowers in July and August. 'Summer Beauty' begins growing very early in the season and keeps clean, elegant foliage throughout the summer. Because it's a sterile selection, there's no need to worry about rambunctious self-sowing. 'Summer Beauty' resists insect pests and diseases, is long-lived, and can form an extensive ground cover over time. Hardy to Zone 4. 18"–20" tall × 6"–10" wide.

### Cypress spurge

*Euphorbia cyparissias*

Its small size and texture resembling blue-spruce needles make cypress spurge a winner for filling in between grasses, as shown here. Cypress spurge forms an exuberant mat of herbaceous, blue-green leaves. From late spring to midsummer, it produces chartreuse blooms. The plant often turns orange in poor soils. In some climates, it's considered invasive. Hardy to Zone 4. 8"–16" tall × indefinite width.

### Common milkweed

*Asclepias syriaca*

Although some catalog descriptions of the plant include the adjectives *rough, coarse,* and *weedy,* common milkweed's outsize leaves, upright habit, rose flowers, and showy fruit make it a good candidate where an architectural plant is needed for a full sun location with poor soil. Its fragrant, umbel-shaped flowers are monarch magnets. It spreads by seeds and rhizomes and is best planted where hot and somewhat dry conditions will keep it in check (as will removing the seedpods before they split). A less rampant, but equally butterfly-friendly milkweed is Sullivant's milkweed (*Asclepias sullivantii*), a brother to common milkweed, which creeps more slowly by rhizomes than its sibling does. Hardy to Zone 3. 3'–5' tall × 1' wide.

## designer tips

### Mastering Rattlesnakes and Milkweeds

When designing a garden with robust and well-adapted plants, remember that they will require thinning because of their happiness with their situation. In this arrangement, Julie Siegel reminds us that plants like rattlesnake master and common milkweed will grow into masses unless you pull some of them out vigilantly once a year.

# THE SILVER MEDAL FOR DEERPROOFING

*Pungent* might be the best word to describe this strongly scented and remarkably silvery combination. "I think they smell great," says designer David Salman, "but my wife, Ava, thinks otherwise when I come back into the house after pruning these plants." Regardless of what humans think of the smell, deer and rabbits find both of these plants equally distasteful. As Salman explains, "Nothing is going to munch these." Both plants come from genera (*Salvia* and *Artemisia*) known for their deer and rabbit resistance, but these two plants also have great aesthetic appeal in the garden. As hinted at by their silver foliage, both of these plants are also heat and drought tolerant in the extreme. Both were chosen for the Plant Select program for their beauty and durability in the Intermountain West.

*Deer and rabbits find both of these plants equally distasteful.*

**Giant-flowered purple sage**
*Salvia pachyphylla*
A newcomer to cultivation, giant-flowered purple sage has had an impact on the garden scene in the West. Colorado seedsman Alan Bradshaw supplied David Salman with the first seeds for this California native plant. The sterling plant with iridescent purple blooms has since appeared in plantings at the Denver Botanical Garden. It will take all the sun and heat you can throw at it, and it prefers well-drained soil. It responds well to a shearing in late summer after it blooms. Hardy to Zone 5. 3' tall × 30" wide.

**Curlicue artemisia**
*Artemisia versicolor* 'Seafoam'
Low, silver, and very aromatic, curlicue artemisia is a fine growing companion to giant-flowered purple sage. Known for its "foamy" curling leaves, curlicue adds a soft, lacy contrast to surrounding plants that are more stiff, upright, and architectural. It's an interesting alternative to the more common 'Powis Castle' artemisia. Hardy to Zone 4. 8" tall × 24" wide.

*designer tips*

## Sage Edging

To repel deer, David Salman recommends planting sage and artemisia in swathes around the perimeter of your garden. "If deer encounter a barrier of unappetizing plants on the border of a garden, it can discourage them from browsing the interior portions of the garden."

# THE HAPPY ACCIDENT: I DID NOT PLANT THIS!

On a sloping hillside plot at Chanticleer in Wayne, Pennsylvania, horticulturist Laurel Voran does not shy away from orange — there are great masses of butterfly weed on this hillside — but sometimes an interloper comes along, making for a happy accident. That was case with this duo, in which sweet William catchfly inserted itself into a large planting of butterfly weed. Laurel exclaims, "I did not plant this! The Silene came in somehow. (Compost? Pant cuffs?) I recognized it as a seedling and knew it would fit the color scheme for the area and so I left it. Now I love it!"

*Letting a few plants grow where they choose can produce some of the most exciting results in your garden.*

**Sweet William catchfly**
*Silene armeria*
The eye-catching clusters of carmine pink flowers in this catchfly rise up to just the right height to mingle effectively with the adjacent butterfly weed. Sweet William catchfly has sticky stems and gray-green basal leaves similar to penstemon leaves. Hardy to Zone 8, but grown as an annual in colder climates. 6" tall × 12" wide.

**Butterfly weed**
*Asclepias tuberosa*
Surely butterfly weed is the poster child of the native gardening movement in the United States. This darling of native plant gardens — with its flaming orange, umbel-shaped flowers; upright form; and bright green, lance-shaped leaves — deserves praise. A tolerance for both drought and deluge and the ability to attract butterflies make it a good choice for naturalistic gardens. It is also a great companion of hot pink to purple, blue, and lavender-colored flowers. Hardy to Zone 4. 36" tall × 12" wide.

*designer tips*

## Be Open to Self-Sowing

The true mark of a great gardener is not just knowing what weeds to pull, but also recognizing what sprouts you should leave alone. Letting a few plants grow where they choose may produce some of the most exciting and surprising results in your garden. Plants like sweet William catchfly may surprise you with their ability to appear not only where they grow best, but also where they look best.

The juxtaposition of two plants — a yellow spirea (*Spiraea* Mellow Yellow) for a vibrant background and deep purple hybrid sage (*Salvia* 'Caradonna'), which sends up purple spires like pickets — makes for an intriguing scene at Linden Hill Gardens in Ottsville, Pennsylvania.

# Yellow Rockets for Boggy Pockets

In a low, damp, Midwest courtyard, designer Julie Siegel faced the challenge of filling a small, rectangular plot in a manner that would be attractive from three sides, because of the way the windowed, U-shaped residence wraps around the area. Because this garden area is a focal point, she also wanted to incorporate plants with four-season interest. As skilled designers often do, she began with a small tree, a multitrunked serviceberry, to provide some height yet not overwhelm the space. The spreading branches of the serviceberry also echo the horizontal architecture of the house, which was designed by a student of Frank Lloyd Wright. Around the serviceberry, Siegel went to work with plants that thrive in damp partial shade, taking care to use a palette with a maximum diversity of leaf sizes. To offset the general damp and shady feel of the site, Siegel used plants with yellow flowers and leaves to enliven the space — suggesting sunlight through her use of yellow and yellow-green foliage. Plants like 'The Rocket' ligularia, yellow flag iris, and a lime-green queen of the meadows brighten what could otherwise feel like a dark and foreboding space.

*Enliven damp and shady sites with yellow flowers.*

### Serviceberry
*Amelanchier canadensis*
This native North American tree makes an attractive central feature in small gardens that are cool and wet. In spring, white-petaled flowers appear and mature into tasty, blueberry-like fruits that are used in jams and pies. Its small size, picturesque branching, and orange-red fall foliage recommend it for areas with medium-wet soils and full sun to part shade. Hardy to Zone 4. 25'–30' tall × 15'–20' wide.

### 'The Rocket' ligularia
*Ligularia stenocephala 'The Rocket'*
Large, heart-shaped, serrated leaves characterize this herbaceous perennial known for its vertical, yellow flowers. Julie Siegel likes this particular cultivar better than the other ligularias because of its highly vertical bloom stalks, which help lift the eyes upward toward the light. An indicator plant, ligularia will let you know immediately when it's thirsty by drooping. 'The Rocket' is a great plant to include with smaller-leaved plants in damp soils. In warm climates, it needs afternoon shade. Hardy to Zone 4. 4' tall × 24" wide.

### Yellow queen of the meadows
*Filipendula ulmaria 'Aurea'*
An easy-to-grow, sunny yellow foliage plant, this queen of the meadows grows in damp full-sun or part-shade conditions. Creamy white flowers add to the allure of its impressive lime-to-gold foliage. Because the cultivar 'Aurea' does not come true from seed, deadheading the seedheads is recommended to avoid seeding a mass of nongolden plants. Hardy to Zone 3. 2'–3' tall × 2'–3' wide.

### Yellow flag
*Iris pseudacorus*
The extremely vertical, 36-inch-long blades of yellow flag contrast nicely with the horizontal leaves of the ligularia in the foreground and provide a strong mid- to late-summer punch of yellow in the garden. Yellow flag is a marginal plant (it likes to grow beside water) and enjoys moist or even waterlogged soil. Good for low spots or pondside plantings. Hardy to Zone 5. 3'–5' tall × 1'–2' wide.

### Hesse cotoneaster
*Cotoneaster × hessei*
Occupying its own slightly raised bed on the sunniest side of the garden, Hesse cotoneaster trails into the yellow queen of the meadows below it. This hybrid is resistant to the fire blight and spider mites that can plague other popular cotoneasters. Its mid-green leaves turn reddish purple in autumn. Hardy to Zone 4. 12"–18" tall × 3' wide.

*designer tips*

## Reinvigorating Queen of the Meadows
If the leaves of your queen of the meadows are looking a little peaked or, heaven forbid, ragged by midsummer, cut back the stems nearly to the ground and you will encourage new growth for fall.

# SPIKES, SPHERES, AND SPIRES

Dryland-garden designers often use cactus and succulents as sculpture, but enrolling perennials as sculptural elements is more unusual. In addition to the round and spiky shapes, purple gayfeather and silver sage make for an icy-cool feel in this vignette. Judiciously, designer Judith Phillips spaces the plants just far enough apart so that the form of each plant can be appreciated on its own. This strategy is not only handsome but is also water-wise. Just creeping into the side of the frame are the awn-shaped seed heads of blue oat grass. In fall, the planting reaches a crescendo, as pictured here, when the gayfeather blooms and the blue oat grass seed heads turn straw colored.

## designer tips

### Keep Your Gayfeather Upright

Because gayfeather is so xeric, Judith Phillips advises holding back on watering. "When it starts shooting up its flower stems in summer, it should be watered sparingly so the plant maintains its form. Too much water sends the lax stems sprawling across the ground."

*Enrolling perennials as sculptural elements gives zing to monotonous beds.*

**'Powis Castle' artemisia**
*Artemisia × 'Powis Castle'*
Tough and well adapted to a wide variety of climates, 'Powis Castle' serves as a splendid backdrop for the purple flowers of gayfeather. Although this tidy, mounding artemisia is common in temperate gardens, it's undeservedly underutilized in southwestern gardens. Because it rarely flowers, 'Powis Castle' generally maintains its rounded appearance without deadheading. It's drought tolerant and not fussy about soil types. Here, it serves as a mounding foil to the otherwise vertical plants in this combination. Hardy to Zone 4. 36" tall × 30" wide.

**Gayfeather**
*Liatris punctata*
Enduring all manner of weather extremes — heat, cold, and humidity — gayfeather is one of Judith Phillips's signature plants, and the species *punctata* is by far her favorite. As Phillips remarks, "It is more compact and drought tolerant than the plains species [*Liatris spicata*]." Hardy to Zone 3. 32" tall × 24" wide.

**Blue oat grass**
*Helictotrichon sempervirens*
This great blue hemisphere of grass is topped with long, stiff, straw-colored seed heads. In this design, the seed heads echo the upright shape of the gayfeather spikes. Plant in full sun and in well-drained, moderately fertile soil. Blue oat grass is a standout among other purple- or silver-leaved plants. Hardy to Zone 4. 3'–4' tall × 24" wide.

# MIXING FIRETAILS WITH RATTLESNAKES

Only three plants comprise this transparent combination designed by Lisa Delplace of Oehme, van Sweden Associates in a naturalistic border in the Lakeside Gardens at Chicago Botanic Garden. The slender knotweed pushes its way up through the rattlesnake master, making for a transparent queue of bright dots of white and hot pink with the coneflowers. Designed for long midsummer color and interest, this highly repeatable palette could be replicated in many full-sun garden situations.

*Plants with tall semitransparent bloom stalks look like floral arrangements.*

**Rattlesnake master**
*Eryngium yuccifolium*
This parsley-family plant sports pale white-green flowers that resemble spiky golf balls and features a sharp rosette of waxy, gray foliage similar to that of yuccas. Native Americans used its roots as a snakebite remedy, hence its common name. In gardens, it's excellent as a specimen or when planted in multiples — which it will do on its own if it's not thinned. Zone 4. 3'–5' tall × 12" wide.

**'Magnus' prairie coneflower**
*Echinacea purpurea* 'Magnus'
Bolder flowers and deep green leaves bring prairie coneflower to the forefront of the vignette. The pink and orange flowers of this tap-rooted prairie plant are the inspiration for this combination. The selection 'Magnus', the 1998 Perennial Plant of the Year, has huge flowers whose petals radiate out flat from the cone. Hardy to Zone 4. 36" tall × 18" wide.

**'Firetail' knotweed**
*Persicaria amplexicaulis* 'Firetail'
All the rage in Europe, this vigorous perennial produces slender, architectural flowers on slight stems over substantial, medium-green foliage. 'Firetail' blooms over a long season — summer to frost — in full sun or partial shade. This cultivar, unlike the straight species, is not invasive. Hardy to Zone 5. 4' tall × 1' wide.

## designer tips

## Mingle Uprights with Uprights

As demonstrated effectively here, mixing two upright growers with different textures is just plain fun. In addition to rattlesnake master, try mixing 'Firetail' knotweed with 'Herbstsonne' coneflower (*Rudbeckia* 'Herbstsonne') and tall verbena (*Verbena bonariensis*).

# SUN AND SKY

This simple yet out-of-the-ordinary design is pared down to two elementals: the brilliant colors of sun and sky. As designer David Salman puts it, "Looking at these two plants is like looking at the sun and sky reflected at ground level." The stems of this goldenrod form a sort of scaffolding for the sometimes-floppy sage. If you like pure undiluted color, this early-fall-blooming duo aims to please.

*Blue- and yellow-flowering plants bring the sun and sky down to ground level.*

**'Fireworks' goldenrod**
*Solidago rugosa* 'Fireworks'
This plant is so easy to grow that David Salman describes it as a "no-brainer." The well-mannered goldenrod has very architectural, downward arching blooms that resemble the arching tails of a Fourth of July display. It also overcomes two of the common objections to planting goldenrod in a garden: it's sterile, and therefore not weedy, and because it's not wind pollinated, it's non-allergenic. Hardy to Zone 5. 36" tall × 24" wide.

**Pitcher's blue sage**
*Salvia pitcheri* 'Grandiflora'
No doubt about it — Pitcher's blue sage is a lanky plant, but its prolific, sky-blue flowers in fall make it the perfect companion for goldenrod. The form of Pitcher's blue sage is greatly improved by pinching it back in the late spring. If you grow this plant solo, you may want to stake it or provide other support. Hardy to Zone 4. 4' tall × 24" wide.

*designer tips*

## Place Goldenrod and Sage beneath Deciduous Trees

This combo is an excellent choice to plant beneath spring-blooming trees so that the garden is interesting in the early part of the season before the Pitcher's blue sage and 'Fireworks' goldenrod really get growing. David Salman suggests planting them beneath Sargent crab apples (*Malus sargentii*) or other spring bloomers.

# TWEAKING THE CONEFLOWER

Every once in a while, the plant breeders hit a home run and come up with a really beautiful and useful new cultivar, like the dwarf coneflower 'Pixie Meadowbrite'. The result of Dr. Jim Ault's breeding at Chicago Botanic Gardens, it is the child star in this combination featuring plants that exhibit generous summer color with minimal fuss. Designed by Lisa Delplace of Oehme, van Sweden Associates in a naturalistic border in the Lakeside Gardens at Chicago Botanic Garden, this design demonstrates that you don't need exotic plants to make a great display. You need just one well-bred coneflower, a couple of exceptional daylily cultivars, and patch of lamb's ears for a cheerful, long-blooming bed.

## designer tips

### Breeding for Stature

With the shrinking size of new gardens, plant breeders and collectors are clamoring to find new small cultivars. Browse the Web sites of groups like the North American Rock Garden Society, breeders like Proven Winners, or online catalogs (see Resources, page 229) to find new diminutive plants. Try searching for the terms *tiny*, *pixie*, *petite*, and *dwarf* to find new cultivars.

**'Pixie Meadowbrite' coneflower**
*Echinacea* 'Pixie Meadowbrite'
This new cultivar was developed at the Chicago Botanic Gardens and is the most compact coneflower on the market. Because of its short stature, it can be used more often in small garden spaces and even toward the front of a bed without fear of it obstructing other plants. It could even serve as a ground cover. A long bloom time and numerous flowers make 'Pixie Meadowbrite' perfect for gardeners who once considered other coneflowers too gangly for their small spaces. Hardy to Zone 4. 18"–20" tall × 24" wide.

**'Mary Todd' daylily**
*Hemerocallis* 'Mary Todd'
This is one large-flowered, yellow daylily that will grow in a variety of soil types and is disease resistant as well. Here, it forms the backdrop for the lower coneflowers and lamb's ears. Full sun to part shade. Hardy to Zone 3. 26" tall × 20" wide.

**'Lady Fingers' daylily**
*Hemerocallis* 'Lady Fingers'
A vigorous, award-winning plant, this spider-shaped daylily has great six-inch, yellow-green flowers with twisted, recurving petals borne on thin stems. Hardy to Zone 2. 29"–31" tall × 29"–35" wide.

**'Big Ears' lamb's ears**
*Stachys byzantina* 'Big Ears'
'Big Ears' (also sold as 'Helene von Stein') lamb's ears is a workhorse, and its soft leaves help mediate between the pink of the coneflowers and yellow of the daylilies. This cultivar is more tolerant of high humidity, is less prone to summer dieback, and doesn't bloom — a bonus to gardeners who grow lamb's ears for the foliage alone. Hardy to Zone 4. 10" tall × 24" wide.

# RISING FROM THE GRAVEL

Above a floor of blue-gray quarry stone, this combo of 'East Friesland' sage, 'Transparent' tall purple moor grass, and dwarf lilac form an exuberant, pathside planting in Duncan Brine's New York garden. Because the plants are spaced generously, they can be appreciated both on their own and as part of a larger design. Moundlike perennials rising from gravel are one of Duncan Brine's specialties. The purple, vertical spires of 'East Friesland' sage in the foreground contrast with the nearby arching leaves of purple moor grass. There's a subtle distinction between the highlight on the lustrous, linear leaves of the grass and the matte leaves of the dwarf Korean lilac. Between and just behind the center line of the lilacs, there's a subtle brightening in the background provided by the green and cream of a dwarf weigela.

## Create Borderless Beds with Gravel

Many things can be said about Duncan Brine's large, naturalistic garden, but one thing that cannot be said is that he is stingy with rock mulch. "I use a lot of gravel," he confesses. In fact, the liberal use of rock is an important part of his design scheme, allowing the pathways and garden beds to meet without an edge. This "edgeless" method is practical to maintain and aesthetically effective, giving appropriate focus to the plants surrounded by gravel. The Brine garden utilizes natural, rounded gravel, hauled in from a local quarry, in a variety of sizes and with subtle color differences.

### 'East Friesland' sage
*Salvia nemorosa* 'East Friesland'
This is a sage worth deadheading. With vigilance, you'll find it's one of the longest-blooming perennials, summer through fall, when its eye-catching flowers persist. More compact and tidy than its parent *Salvia nemorosa*. Hardy to Zone 5. 18" tall × 18" wide.

### 'Transparent' tall purple moor grass
*Molinia caerulea* subsp. *arundinacea* 'Transparent'
The shiny, arching leaves of purple moor grass provide good foliar contrast to the bolt upright shape of the sage. Although it blooms later in summer, the long, vertical, leafless, flowering stems of the grass echo the verticality of the salvia. Purple moor grass likes moist, well-drained soil. Hardy to Zone 5. 5' tall × 24" wide.

### Dwarf Korean lilac
*Syringa meyeri* 'Palibin'
The rounded outline of the lilac is formal and useful as a structuring element, playing the role of "flowering" boxwood. In full sun, it's dense and able to lightly rebloom on new, delicate branches. Although this dwarf lilac is outstanding as a formal addition, its uniform shape could spoil the look of a loose, naturalistic area. In dry, part shade, however, this dwarf lilac is much more open and can be considered a transitional shrub, spanning formal and natural areas. Hardy to Zone 4. 5' tall × 4' wide.

*Gravel mulch allows pathways and garden beds to meet without an edge.*

# LATE SUMMER IS FOR BUTTERFLIES

Late summer is one of the most overlooked times in the perennial garden. Enter 'Magnus' prairie coneflower and 'Rotkugel' ornamental oregano. This easygoing pair, with one towering plant and one low-grower, provides a consistent late-summer to fall show with minimal fuss. As David Salman says, "Both of these plants are versatile and long blooming. They don't require any special soil and only need to be cut back once in early spring." As an added bonus, the copious nectar from both of these plants attracts monarch and painted lady butterflies.

*A consistent late-summer show with minimal fuss*

### 'Rotkugel' ornamental oregano
*Origanum* × 'Rotkugel'
Introduced to the United States by Dan Hinkley, a plantsman from Washington state, this very floriferous oregano forms low, rolling mounds of foliage. The large sprays of bicolored pink-and-purple flowers bloom August through October and attract scads of butterflies. Because it grows from stolons, it's easily propagated from root divisions. Hardy to Zone 5. 15" tall × 18" wide.

### 'Magnus' purple coneflower
*Echinacea purpurea* 'Magnus'
Among the many coneflower cultivars, 'Magnus' stands out for its giant flowers whose petals are held out flat rather than drooping, as is typical of most coneflowers. The Perennial Plant Association chose this vivid and vigorous plant as the 1998 Perennial Plant of the Year. Hardy to Zone 4. 36" tall × 18" wide.

## designer tips

### Plant Spring Bulbs with This Combo
To jazz up this perennial couple early in spring, use a variety of bulbs: daffodils, Siberian squill, yellow Darwin tulips, and crocus. Try 'Ruby Giant' crocus (*Crocus tommasinianus* 'Ruby Giant'), a ground-squirrel-resistant variety with large purple flowers; quail daffodil (*Narcissus* 'Quail'), a fragrant and very floriferous golden daff; *Tulipa tarda*, a low-growing, yellow, star-shaped tulip that spreads like a ground cover; and Siberian squill (*Scilla siberica* 'Spring Beauty'), a ready reseeder that is good for tucking beneath the oregano and coneflowers.

# Buckwheat Select

This plant pairing uses a design trick that works nearly every time. Take a low-growing, mat-forming plant, sidle it up against a strong, upright grower with a contrasting flower color and foliage, and you'll be treated to a powerful effect. In this case, two durable Rocky Mountain plants — a spectacular, glowing buckwheat called Kannah Creek and a canyon penstemon — are the stars of a show acted out in vivid yellow and hot pink, with white native fleabane as a bit player. This assortment is nestled into a slope of Colorado horticulturist Panayoti Kelaidis's Denver garden.

*A glowing buckwheat and a canyon penstemon*

### Kannah Creek buckwheat

*Eriogonum umbellatum* var. *aureum* 'Psdowns' (Kannah Creek)

Panayoti Kelaidis is well known as a plant explorer: a man who finds an exceptional plant in the wild, introduces it to horticulture, and shines a bright spotlight on it. This is what he helped do with Kannah Creek buckwheat, a mat-forming ground cover from Colorado's Grand Mesa known for masses of yellow, popcorn-shaped flowers that appear to hover over the plant on wiry stems. Kannah Creek, chosen for the Plant Select program, is distinguished from other sulphur buckwheats by its brighter yellow flowers and foliage that turns purple-red in autumn and winter. Adaptable to a wide range of soil conditions, including clay, as long as reasonably good drainage is provided. Hardy to Zone 3. 12"–15" tall × 12"–24" wide.

### Canyon penstemon

*Penstemon pseudospectabilis*

Handsome, triangular, toothed leaves and towering, hot pink flower spires characterize this rugged southwestern native. In spring to early summer, hummingbirds visit the tubular flowers; later, the plant produces copious seed. Cutting back the spent bloom stalks (and collecting seed!) keeps the plant's rosette tidy when it's out of bloom. Needs good drainage and full sun to part shade. Hardy to Zone 5. 1'–3' tall × 1'–2' wide.

## designer tips

## Learn Design from Your Plants

When asked about his design methods, Panayoti Kelaidis remarks, "I don't design; the plants design themselves. They teach you, and then you learn. The plants either die or they thrive and prosper, and in this way, you learn which plants like to be next to each other. Your role is to aid and abet what works." One advantage of designing in this way is that successful combinations, like Kannah Creek buckwheat and canyon penstemon, flourish and repeat themselves serendipitously throughout the garden.

# Short Stuff International

Of this handsome mix of Old World and New World characters, designer David Salman says, "I love this combination of plants. I use the pure orange of the pineleaf penstemon against the blue of lavender all the time." Although the American pineleaf penstemon and 'England' hybrid lavender are the major players here, the bit parts are doled out to the vigorous coreopsis 'Zagreb' (named for the Croatian capital city) and the wandlike spires of elfin pink penstemon. What David doesn't mention is that all of these plants are compact and could be wedged into all but the most restricted of spaces.

### designer tips

## Build Berms for Sharper Drainage

Although these species are not picky about soils, plants in the *Lavandula* and *Penstemon* genera are notorious lovers of fast-draining (what the English call "sharp") soils. In heavy clays and other slow-draining soils, David Salman recommends adding a 50/50 mix of coarse sand and ⅜-inch screened gravel to existing soil (in a 1-to-1 ratio) to make berms for plants that enjoy quick drainage.

*Pure orange against lavender*

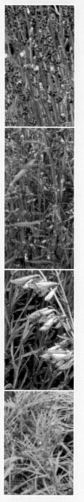

### 'England' hybrid lavender
*Lavandula* ✕ 'England'
Although there are gardeners who are resentful because they can't grow it, almost no one dislikes lavender. For pure visual appeal, with its silvery foliage and dark blue flowers, 'England' might be the most handsome lavender you'll ever find. In addition to its admirable form, it is notably fragrant, very heat tolerant, and distasteful to rabbits and deer. Hardy to Zone 6. 15"–18" tall × 15"–18" wide.

### Pineleaf penstemon
*Penstemon pinifolius*
The American counterpart to 'England' lavender, pineleaf penstemon is a tough Arizona and New Mexico native (from the coldest parts of those states) whose fine, needlelike foliage is topped with flaming orange flowers for six to eight weeks in midsummer. As the mature stems of pineleaf penstemon become woody, the bright green foliage becomes what David Salman calls "an attractive evergreen shrublet." Hardy to Zone 4. 18" tall × 12" wide.

### 'Elfin Pink' beardtongue
*Penstemon barbatus* 'Elfin Pink'
This reliable selection adds bright pink spires to the midsummer garden, and the basal rosette of its evergreen foliage is attractive throughout the year. In this combination, the beardtongue lends an unexpected splash of pink; 'Elfin Pink' has a softening effect on the stronger blues, oranges, and yellows that surround it. Hardy to Zone 4. 24" tall × 15" wide.

### 'Zagreb' tickseed
*Coreopsis verticillata* 'Zagreb'
This stout little coreopsis hunkers down at the front of this combination, providing a burst of gold at the front of the border. Particularly in colder zones, 'Zagreb' is the cultivar of choice because it breaks dormancy several weeks earlier than other popular tickseeds such as 'Moonbeam'. Hardy to Zone 3. 12" tall × 18" wide.

Simplicity is often the
essence of good design,
as this duo of garden
phlox (*Phlox panicu-
lata*) and Russian sage
(*Perovskia atriplicifolia*)
proves in Jan Barbo's
New Mexico garden.

# Rugged Trio for Dry Spots

In the relatively cold-winter, high-desert gardens that are Judith Phillips' specialty, providing seasonal interest is no small challenge. In this front-yard combo, she mixes bold, oval-shaped prickly pear with buckwheat and a low, mat-forming Greek germander. Like sculpture, the prickly pear guarantees year-round structure, while the buckwheat and germander add seasonal changes. These allies are extremely tough and can be grown with little or no irrigation, even in harsh arid climates. The elements of rock-garden design (space between plants, rock mulches) that Phillips employs add a minimalist look that works well with contemporary or Southwest-themed architecture.

### Engelmann's prickly pear
*Opuntia engelmannii*
Engelmann's prickly pear is a common and tenacious plant in most of the Southwest. In spring, showy yellow flowers appear. In late summer, its bright red fruit can be harvested and made into juice, jelly, or candy. For colder climates, try the smaller beavertail cactus (*Opuntia basilaris*), which blooms shocking pink flowers. In wetter eastern climes, use *Opuntia humifusa*, which is hardy to Zone 5. Engelmann's is hardy to Zone 8. 6' tall × 10' wide.

### Wright's buckwheat
*Eriogonum wrightii*
A rugged plant that is well adapted to a variety of conditions, including extreme cold and aridity, Wright's buckwheat is found growing on mountaintops as high as 11,000 feet. Its silvery gray foliage and white to light pink flowers are only part of the story. Its narrow, strawlike stems are a nice textural contrast. A true garden gem. Hardy to Zone 6. 1.5' tall × 2' wide.

### Greek germander
*Teucrium aroanium*
Felt-covered, gray leaves and lavender flowers characterize this creeping ground cover that thrives in poor, rocky soils. Provide full sun and good drainage. Hardy to Zone 6. 6" tall x 4' wide.

## designer tips

## Plant for Seasonal Transitions

Although many parts of the country don't experience the sort of dramatic seasonal changes that occur in New England, there are subtle seasonal shifts that make the garden plants interesting. Regarding this combination, Judith Phillips says, "I particularly enjoy the transitions through the seasons — when the germander first starts to bloom and well into summer, when the buckwheat is a mass of threadlike silver stems. It's a nice contrast to both the germander and the cactus. Then the buckwheat and germander blooms contrast with the cactus fruit. Later in autumn, the buckwheat seed heads become a rusty orange. Even in winter, there is color — silver leaves and stems against the dull-green cactus pads."

# Fire Kings and White Dragons

When I first stepped into the Smithsonian's Ripley Garden, I was magnetically attracted to this central bed of orange, apricot, and blue. There is something wonderfully bold and unfussy about the combination that says, "You're not in granny's garden anymore." I concluded that the bed is a great study in saturated color. Orange and blue are opposites on the color wheel, and when they are intermingled, as they are here — at full strength — the effect is outstanding. The formula is simple: two shades of orange lilies mixed with annual larkspur, a clump of Siberian iris up front, and maiden grass and fleece flower backing up everything. Horticulturist Janet Draper has put lots of time into getting this combo just right. She remarks, "It is really challenging to keep the scheme going, and it has taught me a lot about the differences in blue and lavender! We all need a challenge!"

*You're not in granny's garden anymore.*

*designer tips*

## Add Burgundy Annuals to Orange- and Blue-Flowering Plants

To help keep the blue and orange grouping lively, Janet Draper sometimes buttresses blue and orange with dark-colored plants. "I've found that the addition of a bit of burgundy really helps," she says. Draper suggests mixing in bronze fennel and black cotton (*Foeniculum vulgare* 'Purpureum' and *Gossypium herbaceum* 'Nigra') with this planting.

### 'Fire King' Asiatic lily
*Lilium* 'Fire King'

'Fire King' is not some newfangled lily but rather a vibrant old-fashioned plant repurposed here for a bold effect. The intensity of its orange flowers, which are displayed on upright stems from late spring through early summer, is formidable. Prefers full sun with mulch around the roots and regular watering. Hardy to Zone 3. 30" tall × 18"–24" wide.

### 'Menton' Asiatic Lily
*Lilium* 'Menton'

This cultivar is equal to 'Fire King' in every way, except that it blooms apricot-colored flowers rather than deep orange ones. Having two shades of orange adds depth to the grouping. Likes full sun with mulch around the roots and regular watering. Hardy to Zone 3. 32" tall × 18"–24" wide.

### Larkspur
*Consolida ambigua*

Slender, ferny, and — above all — blue, larkspur is sometimes called "the poor man's delphinium," but in this combo, and in any garden aiming for an informal cottage look, it fits the bill perfectly, providing vertical blue spires in early summer. Larkspur is available in light blue, electric blue, white, and pink and in single or double varieties, but this design calls for straight electric blue. Plant from seed in the fall in the South and in early spring in colder regions. Annual. 24"–36" tall × 6"–8" wide.

### 'Cabaret' maiden grass
*Miscanthus sinensis* 'Cabaret'

A freestanding specimen here, 'Cabaret' provides an arching geyser of a plant at the back of this border. It is also useful for summer screening or waterside plantings. Aggressive reseeding is sometimes a problem, but Janet Draper says, "Since it blooms *very* late, and seeds do not normally mature in our area [Washington, D.C.], we do not have a self-sowing problem." Hardy to Zone 6. 6' tall × 4' wide.

### Siberian iris
*Iris sibirica*

Even out of bloom, Siberian iris plays an important role in this huddle of plants. The bright green, swordlike leaves of Siberian iris echo the blades of the 'Cabaret' maiden grass in the background. When in bloom, its blue-violet flowers continue the orange and blue theme. Give plants full sun with good drainage. Hardy to Zone 3. 20"–48" tall × 18" wide.

### White dragon knotweed
*Persicaria polymorpha*

White dragon knotweed is another tall background plant. Its plumy flowers lend a soft, lacy feel to the rear of the mix, blooming from early to midsummer. Though it tolerates partial shade, it achieves maximum height and a nice vase shape in full sun. Hardy to Zone 3. 5' tall × 24" wide.

# GET LOOSE WITH YOUR PLANTING STYLE

When walking among ornamental meadow grasses, there is nothing more exciting than happening onto a hummock of jewel-like prairie flowers. At Neil Diboll's garden, this tough trio of gold, orange, and white emerges like a gift from the grasslands — the very picture of pretty informality. Although the planting is informal, it did not happen spontaneously (see Kill, Mow, Burn).

### Butterfly weed
*Asclepias tuberosa*
Surely the butterfly weed is the poster child of the native gardening movement in the United States. This darling of native plant gardens, with its flaming orange, umbel-shaped flowers and bright green, lance-shaped leaves, deserves praise. A tolerance for drought and deluge and, true to its name, the ability to attract butterflies make it a good choice for naturalistic gardens. Hardy to Zone 4. 36" tall × 12" wide.

### Black-eyed Susan
*Rudbeckia hirta*
This longtime favorite plains biennial is fast growing and simple to start from seed. Because it blooms the second year from seed, it's a good choice for color while you wait for longer-lived perennials to fill in. Hardy to Zone 3. 12"–36" tall × 12" wide.

### White prairie clover
*Dalea candida*
This slender grower has showy, buttonlike flowers on skinny stems that list over into adjacent plants. Its pure white flowers open from June through September and are visited by bees and butterflies. Like other legumes, it has nodules on its roots (mycorrhizae) that fix nitrogen in the soil. Full sun, adaptable to many soils, and a great companion for larger-flowered perennials. Hardy to Zone 4. 3'–4' tall × 2' wide.

## designer tips

## Kill, Mow, Burn

If your vision of planting a prairie garden includes strolling around in a sun bonnet, lazily scattering seeds here and there and waiting for blooms, you may be disappointed to learn that it's a lot more like regular gardening than you thought. In fact, controlling weeds before and after planting is important. A combination of smothering, cultivation, and herbicides may be needed to kill entrenched weeds. After planting, the prairie can be mowed frequently during the first year (to a height of six inches) to prevent weeds from producing more seed while the wildflowers and grasses are less than six inches high. Once the grasses have filled in and the weeds are in check, burning (where allowed) every two to three years will keep your meadow in good shape. After establishment, it does become more carefree. As Diboll remarks, once the grasses and flowers fill in and cover up the soil surface, "all the seats are taken and the plants are doing the work for you."

# UNDER THE ULMUS

In the shadow of the Smithsonian's Arts and Industries building lies what might be the best garden in the capitol city. The Ripley Garden, transformed by the hands of horticulturist Janet Draper, veritably sings with bold plantings. The garden, a series of raised, undulating, curvilinear, brick beds, reveals surprises around every curve. In this combination, I was wooed by the soft, feminine planting that is tailor-made for the shade of an American elm. The pink hydrangea and golden Hakone grass play off the 'Halcyon' hosta, whose cooler blue-green leaves tone down the pink and yellow.

*A soft, feminine planting, tailor-made for the shade*

**'Halcyon' hosta**
*Hosta* 'Halcyon'
Travel to any garden in the South and you're sure to find lots of hostas. The trick to keeping hosta plantings interesting is to mix them with contrasting companions and choose cultivars that are a little out of the ordinary. Although 'Halcyon' is instantly recognized as a hosta by its heart-shaped leaves, the glaucous gray-blue of its foliage distinguishes it from plainer cultivars and makes it a perfect companion for brighter colored plants. Hardy to Zone 3. 14" tall × 28" wide.

**Golden hakone grass**
*Hakonechloa macra* 'Aureola'
This awesome little yellow and green striped grass enlivens shady plantings beneath trees. The multidirectional, weeping leaves, which become tinged with red in the fall, are its chief assets. Hardy to Zone 5. 14" tall × 16" wide.

**'Amethyst' hydrangea**
*Hydrangea macrophylla* 'Amethyst'
The chunky, pink mop heads of 'Amethyst' rise above the surrounding plants and make a nice transition from the elm to the golden hakone grass. Rounded shape and a long bloom season make this cultivar a good choice for shady areas. By adjusting the soil pH, the flower color can be changed to light blue (see Pink, Blue, or White?). Hardy to Zone 6. 5' tall × 5' wide.

## designer tips

### Pink, Blue, or White? Choose Your Hydrangea Color

As well turned out as this assortment is, Janet Draper laments that "the entire combination would be so much better if I would remember to adjust the pH yearly to make the hydrangea blue!" The flower color of pink and blue hydrangeas is dependent on soil acidity and the availability of aluminum in the soil. In acid soils, hydrangeas bloom blue; in alkaline soil (a pH above 6.0), they bloom pink. To make your pink hydrangeas bluer, add sulfur (one to two pounds per 100 square feet, depending on your soil type).

Draper also thinks a white hydrangea such as *H. arborescens* 'Annabelle' would be a good alternative here. The white-flowered hydrangeas don't change color because of differences in soil pH.

# CITY TOWERS AND PRAIRIE POWER

Rising up against the Chicago skyline, the bold yellow spires of compass plant integrate this prairie planting into a city setting in this wild, inspired, Piet Oudolf design at Chicago's Lurie Garden. This simple planting is provocative for its use of three prairie plants: compass plant, rattlesnake master, and a native that has been fiddled with, 'Green Edge' coneflower. If you stand in Oudolf's Lurie Garden, the hordes of butterflies and prairie plants can be disorienting. You might forget that downtown Chicago is 100 yards away; by this token, many city dwellers could reap the benefits of a few well-placed prairie plants in an urban setting. Here, Oudolf takes the native palette (60 percent of the Lurie Garden plant palette comprises prairie natives) and gives it a designer twist by including white coneflowers, rather than the more-common pink variety.

### Compass plant
*Silphium laciniatum*

Compass plant is a tall, sturdy prairie plant that is at home in clay soils. It gets its name because its deeply lobed basal leaves orient themselves on a north–south axis. At maturity, it sends up a massive flower stalk from a rosette that is festooned with as many as a hundred bright yellow, daisylike flowers. Compass plant flowers June through September, followed by ripening seeds that are sought out by birds. In residential gardens, compass plant would be at home at the back of a border, as an accent plant in a cottage garden, or left to naturalize in a prairie garden setting, though it may not bloom until its second or third year in the garden. Hardy to Zone 3. 5'–9' tall × 1.5'–3' wide.

### 'Green Edge' coneflower
*Echinacea purpurea* 'Green Edge'

This white variety with a hint of green in the petals and a strong yellow-green eye grows a little shorter than the pink types and is perfect here in the foreground with compass plant and rattlesnake master. Prefers full sun and average soil. Like the compass plant, 'Green Edge' is an excellent choice for prairie or meadow plantings. Hardy to Zone 3. 30" tall × 12" wide.

### Rattlesnake master
*Eryngium yuccifolium*

This parsley-family plant features pale white-green flowers that resemble spiky golf balls. Its sharp rosette of waxy, gray foliage looks similar to that of yuccas. Native Americans used its roots as a snakebite remedy. In gardens, it's an excellent specimen plant, but it's also effective when planted en masse (which it will do on its own if it's not thinned). In this combination, its spiky globes occupy a spot at the base of the compass plant. Hardy to Zone 4. 3'–5' × 12" wide.

## designer tips

## Other Companions for Compass Plants

In addition to 'Green Edge' coneflower, compass plant can also be combined with the ornamental grass big bluestem (*Andropogon gerardii*), gray coneflower (*Ratibida pinnata*), spiderwort (*Tradescantia* spp.), and woody buddies like New Jersey tea (*Ceanothus americanus*).

Designer Plant Combinations     **Perennial Partners**

# High-Bred Purple Sage and Royal Yarrow

Russian sage and yarrow are perfectly adapted to gardens in the Intermountain West. Some yarrows are perhaps *too* well adapted, causing some gardeners to lament the promiscuous tendencies of the lovely, yellow-flowered plants. In this bold combo, David Salman combines the best and tamest cultivars to create a one-two punch of deep purple-blue and bright yellow that mostly stay where they are put. If you're tired of washed-out pastels that remind you of Victorian lace and gardenias, this combo will turn up the color volume in your garden. If there was ever a great combo for the beginning gardener, this is it; success is very nearly guaranteed with these two hardy and reliable plants.

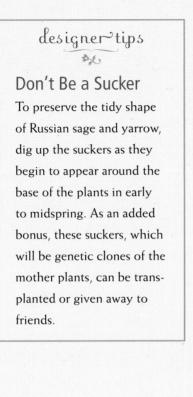

*designer tips*

## Don't Be a Sucker

To preserve the tidy shape of Russian sage and yarrow, dig up the suckers as they begin to appear around the base of the plants in early to midspring. As an added bonus, these suckers, which will be genetic clones of the mother plants, can be transplanted or given away to friends.

### 'Coronation Gold' yarrow
*Achillea filipendulina* 'Coronation Gold'

When it comes to yarrows, 'Coronation Gold' is, as David Salman remarks, "simply the best." Common yarrows have a well-deserved reputation as garden thugs for their proclivity to reseed where you don't want them to, but 'Coronation Gold', which is sterile, is a breed apart. It's also a strong rebloomer, with its intensely gold flowers rising up from delicate, ferny foliage. Unlike taller, seed-grown varieties, 'Coronation Gold' won't crowd out its smaller neighbors. It also has one up on the popular cultivar 'Moonshine', whose flowers are much more muted. In fact, the term "screaming yellow" comes to mind when looking at the umbrella-shaped flower heads. Hardy to Zone 3. 36" tall × 24" wide.

### 'Blue Spire' Russian sage
*Perovskia atriplicifolia* 'Blue Spire'

A quintessential drought-tolerant perennial, Russian sage has quickly become a garden staple in the xeriscapes of the Intermountain West. 'Blue Spire' is a European introduction with deep purple-blue flowers and a uniform, upright shape. Unlike some Russian sage cultivars whose flowers are a mere powder blue, 'Blue Spire' has enough depth and saturation to stand proudly beside 'Coronation Gold.' Tolerant of all soil types including clay, 'Blue Spire' is a truly outstanding perennial. Hardy to Zone 4. 4' tall × 4' wide.

*A one-two punch of deep purple-blue and bright yellow*

# MASSES OF
## *Grasses*

Garden designers in every region of the country are gaga for ornamental grasses, whether they're using the silken threads of Mexican feather grass (*Nassella tenuissima*) or the coarser, metallic blue 'Heavy Metal' switchgrass (*Panicum virgatum* 'Heavy Metal').

Fueling interest in grasses is the movement to include prairie plants in landscape design. Because wild prairie landscapes are composed of about 75 percent grass species, grasses are getting well-deserved attention in prairie-style plantings. Although grasses are often evocative of the prairies, their reach (and natural habitat) extends far beyond the American Midwest. Grasses soften stiff or formal plantings through the introduction of movement and dynamism. They mark a shift in gardening attitudes as well — they seem to allow, by their very unclipped grassiness, an element of wildness to creep into our gardens. They appear, in a word, spontaneous. Grasses, ranging from petite to enormous, can provide transparency or enclosure. The transparent species enable gardeners to plant in and around them. Another way of using grasses, which has been incorporated extensively by Dutch designer Piet Oudolf, is to plant them in great sweeping patterns with perennials to enliven the grasscape seasonally.

It should be noted that the grasses featured in these combinations are mostly clump-forming ornamental grasses that do not have to be mowed (unless you have a whole meadow of them), but rather are cut back (usually only once a year after they're fully established) and are therefore fairly easy to maintain in home gardens. Some ornamental grasses are heavy reseeders and will multiply their numbers if you let them. Special care should be taken not to introduce species that are invasive in your region.

One attribute of ornamental grasses that must be mentioned is winter interest. When properly maintained (cut back in spring rather than in fall), ornamental grasses are among the most compelling plants over the cold months, becoming great white frosty tussocks, icy plumes, and snowy mounds. Even in areas without snow or ice, the winter appearance of tall, tawny stems is arresting; in many warm-climate gardens, tan grass stems are a fine complement to early spring wildflowers.

At Hortulus Farm in Wrightstown, Pennsylvania, a variety of ornamental grasses provide a backdrop for deep pink butterfly weed (*Asclepias*).

# Powered by Blue Oat Grass

Sitting squarely in the middle of the arrangement, blue oat grass is clearly the prima donna of this cool-colored planting. One of the advantages of using blue oat grass as a focal point is the semitransparency of the seed spikes. In this photo, they reveal a gauzy image of the purple spheres of star of Persia on the backside of the grass, while the 'Blue Hill' sage provides a different cool shade of blue.

*designer tips*

## Try Unusual Onions

Plants in the *Allium* genus, like the star of Persia featured here, are notoriously promiscuous interbreeders. The upside of all of this reckless onion sex is the production of many interesting seedlings, with no two exactly like their parents. There are alliums with nodding heads and a variety of bloom colors. Try *Allium* 'Rosy Affair' for a purple-pink variety with a nodding head.

*Seed spikes reveal a gauzy image of purple spheres.*

**Blue oat grass**
*Helictotrichon sempervirens*
A uniform and stiff grass with steely, glaucous leaves, blue oat grass is hard not to love. Because it is so spherical and architectural, it's often used as a substitute for the succulent accent plant sotol (see Fighting Silver with Silver, page 154) in colder climates. Grow in well-drained alkaline soil in full sun. Hardy to Zone 4. 4.5' tall × 24" wide.

**'Blue Hill' sage**
*Salvia × sylvestris* 'Blue Hill'
Although it's dwarfed in size by the adjacent blue oat grass, the spires of 'Blue Hill' are packed with clear blue flowers that contrast with and help show off the blue oat grass. 'Blue Hill' is valued for its compactness and long bloom time. Plant in decent garden soil and provide moderate water for the best performance. Hardy to Zone 4. 15" tall × 18" wide.

**Star of Persia**
*Allium christophii*
The large, eight-inch, metallic purple, spherical flower heads of star of Persia are mostly obscured in this photo, but still they add a magical lavender glow to the backside of the blue oat grass. Star of Persia is a bulb from Turkey with basal foliage (straplike leaves around the base of the plant) and early-summer blooms that are shaped like drumsticks on steroids. After the flower heads go to seed, the dried heads are excellent in flower arrangements. Hardy to Zone 5. 12"–24" tall × 8"–12" wide.

# Nashville White Wedding

This grouping is a great example of the synergy that two special plants can create when they are well married, even if the person who arranged the union did so haphazardly. As designer David Salman comments, "I'm not sure if I even intentionally placed these two plants together, but I was thrilled with the outcome. In fact, they are much better together than they are alone." The resulting effect of David Salman's unwitting matchmaking looks like one thick, grassy, flowering plant that bends in the breeze. Either lining a formal pathway or clustered naturalistically, this combo makes a wispy southern couple.

*This combo makes a wispy southern couple.*

### 'So White' gaura
*Gaura lindheimeri* 'So White'
This variety of the tough and popular gaura is known for the purity of its white flowers, which fade to a pleasing pink. Normally, the flowers are borne on long wandlike stems that move with the wind; when paired with 'Nashville' purple muhly, the result is much more substantial. Hardy to Zone 5. 36" tall × 30" wide.

### Nashville purple muhly
*Muhlenbergia rigida* 'Nashville'
This tough western native is a small, fine-textured grass that sends up copious purple-tan spikes from late summer through fall. In winter, the seed spikes dry to a wheat color. 'Nashville' purple muhly is a switch hitter — able to tolerate conditions ranging from reflected sun to part shade. Hardy to Zone 6. 2' tall × 2' wide.

## designer tips

### Plant a Moon Combination
Although some people consider white flowering gardens snooty, there is no doubt that white flowering plants show up best at night. Try planting white-tufted evening primrose (*Oenothera caespitosa*) beneath the duo shown here for an enhanced and lunar-white effect.

# BLACK, GOLD, AND GREEN

One of my favorite gardens is planted around the late Derek Jarman's fisherman's cottage (which he called Prospect Cottage) on the south coast of England. The garden itself, surrounded by rocky and wild seashore, is riveting, but what makes it even more vibrant is the color scheme of the cottage itself. The clapboard walls are tar-black, while the window and door trim are accented in a bright gold. So when I happened upon this Piet Oudolf ensemble in Battery Park (in New York City), the black-green leaves of Mrs. Robb's bonnet contrasted with the strongly yellow patrinia made me think, "Aha, this is the Prospect Cottage palette in plants."

### Mrs. Robb's bonnet
*Euphorbia amygdaloides var. robbiae*
This dark and vigorous grower is perfect in the dappled shade of the sycamores it is planted under. The glossy, leather leaves make a great foil for the acid-yellow cymes that appear spring to summer. Likes rich, moist soil and filtered light. Hardy to Zone 4. 24" tall × 24"–36" wide.

### 'Goldtau' tufted hair grass
*Deschampsia cespitosa 'Goldtau'*
Backing this combination, 'Goldtau' lends an airy, light feeling to the arrangement, softening the more structural Mrs. Robb's bonnet with its silver and red spikelets that mature gold-yellow. It forms a fine-textured curtain in front of which the other plants can perform. 'Goldtau' is more compact than other hair grass cultivars. Here it contributes greatly to the grassy, woodland feel of this union. Will grow in sun or partial shade and prefers slightly acid soils. Hardy to Zone 5. 30" tall × 30" wide.

### Patrinia
*Patrinia scabiosifolia*
The toothy leaves and upright stems of patrinia help to tie together 'Goldtau' and Mrs. Robb's bonnet. This plant, with its yellow, cup-shaped flowers, has an "herby" sort of appearance and lends much to the wildness of the planting. Likes partial to deep shade and moist, rich soils. Hardy to Zone 5. 3'–7' tall × 24" wide.

*designer tips*

## Celebrate the Seed Head

Once upon a time, the seed heads of garden plants were removed scarcely after (or even before) the flowers faded. With the increasing ecological awareness of the importance of seeds for wildlife, combined with a heightened appreciation for the aesthetics of the seed head itself, gardeners are letting seed heads act like dried-flower arrangements, sometimes enjoying them the entire winter before whacking them back. To best show off tawny and straw-colored seed heads, place them against plants with dark foliage. If they catch light, place them in areas where they can be backlit.

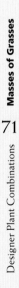

# LAND SHARKS IN THE GRASS

In this Tucson, Arizona, backyard I selected plants with three ideas in mind: movement, color, and structure. Up front, sierra sundrops add an electric yellow vibration that resonates with the seed heads of the Mexican feather grass, while the sturdy sharkskin agave presides over the combination like a land shark. In spite of my high-minded design intentions, I don't have a lot of control over the Mexican feather grass, and I really don't mind if it seeds itself around, because I haven't yet found a plant that doesn't look great next to it. As Henry Mitchell says, "Fortunately, nature has not known how to design plants of really bad or really hideous color, so that even if our own taste is deplorable, we are often saved by the subtlety and grace of the plants we use."

**Mexican feather grass**
*Nassella tenuissima*
Its fine, almost delicate texture belies its true tough-as-nails nature. Although Mexican feather grass is a native of the southwestern United States, it has become a widely used landscape plant, appearing in gardens from California to Massachusetts (where it is used as an annual). In the city of Santa Fe, Mexican feather grass is ubiquitous and seems to have become the self-appointed street-median grass of the city. This speaks to its prodigious reseeding habit, which should not be underestimated. The good news is that Mexican feather grass seedlings are shallow rooted and easily pulled out. Hardy to Zone 5. 2' tall × 2' wide.

**Sierra sundrops**
*Calylophus drummondii*
Sierra sundrops is the brighter, less well-known cousin of regular sundrops (*Calylophus hartwegii* var. *fendleri*). It forms a nice mound and, in late spring, covers itself with chrome yellow, primrose-type blossoms. This high-desert native is very drought tolerant and prefers well-drained soil, although it will tolerate clay if not overwatered. Hardy to Zone 5. 12" tall × 24" wide.

**Sharkskin agave**
*Agave scabra*
Sharkskin agave is a good character; you can plop him down in the middle of perennials and fine-textured grasses and he will be respected instantly, like Tony Soprano walking into an Italian restaurant. As someone who has felt both sharkskin and sharkskin agave leaves, I can vouch for the fact that its leaves truly are the texture of sharkskin. This Chihuahuan Desert native plant likes it hot and dry. It produces lots of offsets (baby sharkskin plants) that can be replanted or given to friends. Its stiff terminal spines can smart, so plant it some distance from well-trodden paths. Hardy to Zone 7. 2'–3' tall × 3'–4' wide.

*designer tips*

## Go with Yellow

Many great plants, particularly in the southwestern part of the United States, are screaming — or buttery or creamy — yellow. A few of my favorite yellows include brittlebush (*Encelia farinosa*), prairie zinnia (*Zinnia grandiflora*), chocolate flower (*Berlandiera lyrata*), and damianita daisy (*Chrysactinia mexicana*).

# LESSONS IN SPANISH ARCHITECTURE

When designer Brandon Tyson goes architectural on you, he doesn't mess around. Rising like the spires of Antoni Gaudi's Catedral de Sagrada Familia in Barcelona, towers of jewels punctuate this planting with very pink exclamation points. In order to spotlight them properly, Tyson provides a dappled, yellow background in the form of a golden locust tree. Below the tower of jewels, the airy seed heads of giant feather grass are just cracking open — as if to provide a layer of mist from which the tower of jewels emerges.

### Tower of jewels
*Echium wildpretii*

Spectacularly conical plants erupt in a cone of pink flowers. Native to the Canary Islands, these biennials grow from a tuft of leaves and appreciate full sun. They are drought tolerant but require moderate water in the low deserts. (See Growing Tower of Jewels for propagating instructions.) Hardy to Zone 10. 6'–8' tall × 1' wide.
*Note:* In colder climates, substitute New England blazing star (*Liatris scariosa* var. *novae-angliae*).

### Golden locust
*Robinia pseudoacacia* 'Frisia'

The lemon-yellow to chartreuse (if grown in shade) pinnate leaves are the main attraction of the golden locust; the intensity of the color is matched by few trees. The size of this locust is controlled easily through pruning. It's very fast growing. Unlike a lot of chartreuse plants, 'Frisia' stays yellow-green all season. Golden locusts, like other members of the genus *Robinia*, sucker freely and, if left unpruned, will make a large multitrunked shrub in hot western climates. In the rest of the country (or when pruned in the West), the golden locust can be a substantial single-trunked tree. Drought and heat tolerant. Hardy to Zone 4. 50' tall × 25' wide.

### Giant feather grass
*Stipa gigantea*

This is a robust evergreen or semi-evergreen perennial grass that sends up purplish spikelets. The leaves are blue-green, linear, and upright. Full sun and well-drained soil. Hardy to Zone 8. 6'–8' tall × 4' wide.
*Note:* In colder climates, substitute 'Heavy Metal' switchgrass (*Panicum virgatum* 'Heavy Metal') for a similar effect.

### Red-yellow kangaroo paw
*Anigozanthos* 'Harmony'

This stunning, tall, evergreen perennial from Australia attracts the attention of humans and hummingbirds. From a base of swordlike leaves, four-to-six-foot red bloom stalks with golden flowers emerge in late spring. Give red-yellow kangaroo paw full sun and well-drained soil. Hardy to Zone 10. 4'–6' tall × 2'–3' wide.
*Note:* In colder climates, substitute yellow hesperaloe (*Hesperaloe parviflora* 'Yellow', hardy to Zone 5).

*designer tips*

## Growing Tower of Jewels

Tower of jewels is a biennial that is best started by seed (seedlings will emerge in 14 to 21 days when temperatures are around 60°F). Echiums reseed freely and have a habit of hybridizing between species with some interesting results. In mild winter areas, sow seed in the ground in fall and protect from severe frost. Plants will take temperatures as low as 23°F.

# THE BILLOWING BORDER

In a wide, sweeping border at Chanticleer in Pennsylvania, Laurel Voran weaves together a subtle and ethereal composition of plants that hover like colored mist above the ground. As Voran remarks, "I picked a very limited number of plants, all with soft textures, and tried to arrange them naturalistically." All of the plants in this mixture prefer full sun and moderate to good drainage. Although the overall effect is reminiscent of heathers of the English moors, these plants tend toward drought tolerance and drier conditions.

### 'White Cloud' calamint

*Calamintha nepeta* 'White Cloud'

'White Cloud' is noted for its tiny, two-lipped, pure white flowers and compact stature. Because the flowers of this calamint are so small, they blend well with the small flowers of Russian sage and delicate panicles of love grass. Like other calamints, it has fragrant foliage and likes good drainage. In warmer climates, *Euphorbia* 'Inneuphdia' (Diamond Frost) can provide a similar effect. Hardy to Zone 4. 18" tall × 24" wide.

### Purple love grass

*Eragrostis spectabilis*

Purple love grass is one of the softest textured plants you can put in a garden, and its airy panicles seem to hover above the grassy foliage. Excellent for naturalistic plantings, this native prefers sandy soil. The spikelets and flowers begin pink-purple and gradually turn a rusty brown. After maturity, the plant has a curious habit: its dried inflorescence will often break free and roll like a tumbleweed into your neighbor's yard or into the next county. Although it is native to much of the United States, in some areas it can be aggressive and invasive. Hardy to Zone 6. 18"–24" tall × 18"–24" wide.

### 'Little Spire' Russian sage

*Perovskia atriplicifolia* 'Little Spire'

A short version of the common and much used Russian sage, 'Little Spire' has white, wiry stems that contrast nicely with the darker surrounding purple love grass. Its lavender-blue spires weep and lean, emphasizing the wild and natural look of the planting. Hardy to Zone 4. 2' tall × 2' wide.

*A very limited number of plants, all with soft textures*

## designer tips

### Select for Effect

Rather than choosing 30 different plants for an area, horticulturist Laurel Voran suggests restricting yourself to seven or fewer plants that complement each other in color and — more important — in texture. After all, seven is the greatest number of objects that the human brain can process instantly without pausing to count.

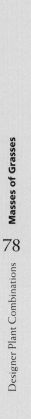

78

Designer Plant Combinations

Like a convention of blue lollipops, globe thistle (*Echinops ritro*) blossoms seem to float when set against the straw-colored threads of Mexican feather grass (*Nassella tenuissima*) in this Santa Fe garden designed by Julia Berman.

# STANDING BEFORE GIANTS

Duncan Brine is not afraid of really large plants. In his six-acre garden, he fills the big spaces with big specimens. In this situation, he squarely faces the question, "What do you plant in front of a 12-foot-tall clump of grass?" The answer, as it turns out, is a pair of rounded willows, a tall ironweed, and a magically glowing, red-pink Korean burnet, all of which serve as members of the giant Chinese silver grass's entourage.

## designer tips

Make a Giant Chinese Silver Grass Circle

Designer Duncan Brine uses giant Chinese silver grass to form a circular screen whose hollow center does double duty as a fort for his children. To make your own silver grass circle, plant seven giant Chinese silver grass plants in a C-shape on a 15-foot-diameter circle.

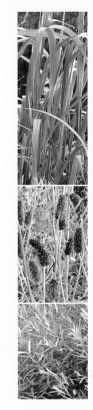

**Giant Chinese silver grass**
*Miscanthus × giganteus*
Shown here in the beginning stages of its growth in early summer, this grass is the tallest, hardiest, non-running grass available. In this grouping, it serves as the backdrop for the rest of the plants. Brine uses giant Chinese silver grass to form a circular screen whose hollow center does double duty as a fort for his children but, from the other side of the pathway, appears simply as a very wide clump of grass. Its girth will increase each year, so make sure to leave plenty of space for this enormous plant. Hardy to Zone 4. 9'–12' tall × 5' wide.

**Korean burnet**
*Sanguisorba tenuifolia 'Purpurea'*
Its slender flower stalks topped with bottlebrush flowers contrast nicely with more densely leaved plants. The flowers are especially attractive when backlit. Korean burnet likes moist soil and may require staking. Hardy to Zone 5. 4'–5' tall × 24" wide.

**'Nana' dwarf purple willow**
*Salix purpurea 'Nana'*
As uniformly shaped as furniture, this dwarf willow, with its steely gray foliage and ball-like form, would seem at home with many different plants. Dwarf purple willow can be cultivated as a low hedge, as well. Hardy to Zone 4. 3' tall × 5' wide.

What do you plant in front of a 12-foot-tall clump of grass?

# RED SMOKE, SAGE, AND GRASSES

There is something alluring about a planting that provides its own backdrop, as this Jonathan Wright–designed Chanticleer arrangement does by growing its own wall of 'Royal Purple' smoke tree and variegated giant reed grass at the back of this bed. There is a sturdy, masculine quality about tall grasses that seems to say, "Ladies (flowers), we've secured the perimeter; feel free to set up shop." The ladies that Wright selects are flashy 'Louie's Orange Delight' sage with an underplanting of 'Compact Red' coleus, both of which provide unity in this vibrant, red-toned planting.

*Create a tapestry by weaving together plants.*

**'Royal Purple' smoke tree**
*Cotinus coggygria* 'Royal Purple'
The purple-green leaves of 'Royal Purple' smoke tree provide a maroon connection to the 'Compact Red' coleus at the front of the border. Its oval leaves turn scarlet in autumn, and its plumelike panicles produce a smoke-like effect in summer, giving the plant its common name. Hardy to Zone 5. 15' tall × 15' wide.

**Variegated giant reed grass**
*Arundo donax* 'Variegata'
A strong, vertical accent with arching, cornlike leaves, variegated giant reed grass is more luminous, compact, and controlled than its nonvariegated brother. Its yellow, white, and green stripes make it a perfect focal point in midsummer. Hardy to Zone 6. 8'–12' tall × 4' wide.

**'Karl Foerster' feather reed grass**
*Calamagrostis × acutiflora* 'Karl Foerster'
The buff seed heads of this durable and well-used perennial grass peek over the top of the daylilies in the foreground. A very reliable ornamental grass with stiff, erect stems. Hardy to Zone 5. 6' tall × 24" wide.

**'Louie's Orange Delight' sage**
*Salvia splendens* 'Louie's Orange Delight'
This vivid, red salvia brings some tropical heat front and center in this set of plants. In hot climates, 'Louie's Orange Delight' prefers afternoon shade. Hardy to Zone 9. 3' tall × 3' wide.

## *designer tips*

## Weave Your Grasses

Horticulturist Jonathan Wright likes creating a tapestry by "weaving" together plants — particularly upright ornamental grasses and perennials. Rather than each plant having its own defined space apart from others, each encroaches on the others by design. The effect — as illustrated here by the 'Louie's Orange Delight' and 'Karl Foerster' — lets flowering plants mingle with semitransparent grasses.

## Silk Tassels and Chardonnay Pearls
## Get a Seal of Approval

In a narrow bed between a wall and sidewalk, Janet Draper assembles some foliar brilliance beneath a 'Sangu Kaku' Japanese maple. Planted in sweeps of variegated Solomon's seal and 'Silk Tassel' grass and punctuated by Chardonnay Pearls, the collection evokes a lively feeling of movement. The design is a great example of how different foliage colors and textures — pearly deutzia, fine silky tassels of grass, and lime and cream Solomon's seal — can carry a planting with very little in the way of conspicuous flowers.

*Different foliage colors and textures can carry a planting with very little in the way of conspicuous flowers.*

### Variegated Solomon's seal

*Polygonatum odoratum 'Variegatum'*

This creeping, rhizomatous perennial is sometimes considered a problem plant because it is so vigorous. That said, Janet Draper remarks, "I have to control the polygonatum, gorgeous thing, because once established it likes to take over. It is easy enough to remove, though, and there are always people that line up for the cast-offs!" In this combination, the white-edged leaves with limey centers light up what might have been an otherwise dark space. In late spring or early summer, variegated Solomon's seal produces creamy pendant flowers along its stems, perfect for a shady woodland border. Hardy to Zone 3. 34" tall × 12" wide.

### 'Silk Tassel' sedge

*Carex morrowii 'Silk Tassel'*

Grown for its very fine-textured blades, 'Silk Tassel' sedge looks indeed a little like the hair of the earth. As this site demonstrates, it is very effective when planted en masse. 'Silk Tassel' sedge likes fertile, moist, well-drained soil in sun or part shade. Hardy to Zone 5. 12" tall × 24" wide.

### Chardonnay Pearls deutzia

*Deutzia gracilis 'Seward'* (Chardonnay Pearls)

Listed as one of *Garden Design* magazine's "Way-Hot 100" plants, the compact, yellow-leaved, and cream-flowered shrub gives a punch of chartreuse and white to this combo. The little, spherical, white buds do look a bit like pearls. Like its companions, Chardonnay Pearls prefers well-drained yet moist soil and part shade — in short, it's a very good woodland garden plant. Hardy to Zone 5. 20"–36" tall × 18"–24" wide.

### August lily

*Hosta plantaginea*

Backing up this display right up against the wall is a colony of August lilies, the most heat tolerant of all the hostas. They also are one of the few fragrant hostas, and in late summer, they send up enormous (at least by hosta standards) six-inch, very fragrant, honeysuckle-scented blooms. An exceptional hosta like this placed against the wall shows Janet Draper's knack for always choosing an interesting plant, regardless of its placement. Hardy to Zone 3. 12–18" tall × 18"–24" wide.

---

*designer tips*

## Add Winter Interest with Evergreens

As attractive as this planting is, Janet Draper is not completely satisfied. She remarks, "This is not a bad combination, but I am improving it by adding evergreens where the August lilies are, since during the winter there is a large bare spot because both the Solomon's seal and August lilies go dormant." Revisiting what you might have considered completed plantings is part of the skill and fun of improving a garden area.

Here, globe thistle (*Echinops ritro*) is interwoven with the variegated blades of *Miscanthus sinensis* 'Variegatus', creating a composition in blue, yellow, and green in this Tom Peace design.

# POOLSIDE BLUES

Beside the crisp geometric edge
of designer Scott Rothenberger's
swimming pool, a path of square-
cut stones skirts the decking.
In and around that decking,
Rothenberger crafts a landscape
of multiple textures that produces
relatively little leaf-litter for the
pool and provides great interest
both in and out of the water.
Anchored by 'Dallas Blues' switchgrass and lined with 'Autumn Joy'
sedum, 'Catlin's Giant' bugleweed,
and lesser calamint, the plant
choices bring a very naturalistic
— almost romantic — feeling
to this otherwise clean-lined
landscape.

*Anchored by
'Dallas Blues'
and lined with
'Autumn Joy'*

### Calamint
*Calamintha nepeta* subsp. *nepeta*

Calamint is planted here for its airy structure and tiny, pure white flowers. Because the flowers of this calamint are so small, it blends well with grasses like 'Dallas Blues'. It has fragrant foliage and likes good drainage. Hardy to Zone 5. 12"–18" tall × 12"–24" wide.

### 'Autumn Joy' sedum
*Sedum 'Autumn Joy'*

With bright green leaves and budded flower heads that look a little like broccoli florets, this showy sedum is hard not to love. In early autumn, it produces flat umbels of deep pink flowers, which mature to coppery brown, providing a long season of interest. Hardy to Zone 3. 2' tall × 2' wide.

### 'Catlin's Giant' bugleweed
*Ajuga 'Catlin's Giant'*

Its distinctive bronze-purple leaves and rhizomatous creeping habit recommend bugleweeds to gardeners looking for good ground covers. 'Catlin's Blue' produces longer (eight-inch), dark blue flower spikes than regular bugleweed and has much larger leaves. Bugleweeds, particularly in arid climates, need part shade to avoid scorching. Hardy to Zone 3. 6" tall × 24" wide.

### 'Dallas Blues' switchgrass
*Panicum virgatum 'Dallas Blues'*

Not only is 'Dallas Blues' the bluest of all the switchgrasses, it is a very adaptable plant, tolerant of high humidity but able to take the heat of arid western climates. Its tassels begin pink and age to tan. 'Dallas Blues' likes full sun and lean, well-drained soil. Give 'Dallas Blues' plenty of room — it is a large, robust plant. Hardy to Zone 5. 4'–6' tall × 18" wide.

### Leyland cypress
× *Cupressocyparis leylandii*

This dense, tapering evergreen tree forms a tall cone shape over time and is a good low-litter plant for poolside plantings. Hardy to Zone 6. 35'–50' tall × 15'–20' wide.

*designer tips*

## Blue Up the 'Dallas Blues'

To intensify the rich blue color of your 'Dallas Blues', give it only infrequent waterings after the plant is established. By watering it only once every seven days during the summer months (assuming there is no rain), you will intensify the blue color and encourage deeper rooting and more drought tolerance.

# TOUGH RASPBERRIES!

Forming a rhythmic grid of color and texture, Mexican feather grass and 'Raspberry Delight' sage are a pair that look great planted en masse in a checkerboard fashion or planted in groups of three, five, or seven. As shown in this David Salman planting, by the time the sage is coming into its full fall splendor, the Mexican feather grass is sporting fine, flaxen seed heads. Earlier in the season, the darker green foliage of 'Raspberry Delight' contrasts well with the lime-green feather grass. This combination is adaptable to small or large plots, is carefree, and uses little water. Even in cities as hot and dry as Tucson, 'Raspberry Delight' and Mexican feather grass thrive on only weekly watering through the summer.

## designer tips

### Plant a Mexican Feather Grass Checkerboard Garden

Use the free-seeding Mexican feather grass to your advantage by planting it in with one or two other flowering perennials in a checkerboard pattern. As the feather grass seeds around and the perennials grow between it, what's formed is a dynamic and exciting quilted design not wholly predetermined by the gardener. In addition to 'Raspberry Delight', consider 'Wild Thing' bush sage (*Salvia greggii* 'Wild Thing'), 'Coral Canyon' twinspur (*Diascia integerrima* 'Coral Canyon'), 'Blue Glow' globe thistle (*Echinops bannaticus* 'Blue Glow'), and 'Homestead Purple' verbena (*Verbena canadensis* 'Homestead Purple').

**'Raspberry Delight' hybrid bush sage**
*Salvia* × 'Raspberry Delight'
This everblooming hybrid proudly holds a profusion of deep-colored, raspberry red flowers above its long, arching branches. It blooms throughout the season, but the flowers are more pronounced in fall and late spring. 'Raspberry Delight' is tolerant of heat and alkaline soil. Hardy to Zone 6, when spring-planted. 3' tall × 3' wide.

**Mexican feather grass**
*Nassella tenuissima*
Its fine, almost delicate texture belies its true tough-as-nails nature. Although Mexican feather grass is a native of the southwestern United States, it has become a widely used landscape plant, appearing in gardens from California to Massachusetts (where it is used as an annual). In the city of Santa Fe, Mexican feather grass is ubiquitous and seems to have become the city's self-appointed street-median grass. This speaks to its prodigious reseeding habit, which should not be underestimated. The good news is that Mexican feather grass seedlings are shallow rooted and easily pulled out. Hardy to Zone 5. 2' tall × 2' wide.

# Brilliant Greens for the Shade

Nothing shows off a designer's prowess more than a group of plants that are all basically some shade of green yet their different forms and textures unite in a dynamic and arresting display. That's what Janet Draper accomplishes in this bed at the Smithsonian's Ripley Garden. The back of the planting is formed by stinking hellebore, autumn fern, and a large variegated hosta. In the foreground, blue-green tufts of 'Silk Tassel' sedge poke their way up through a carpet of golden creeping Jenny. In the middle ground, a yellow toad lily arches gracefully from beneath the hosta.

*Tufts of 'Silk Tassel' sedge poke their way up through a carpet of golden creeping Jenny.*

### designer tips

## Use Bulbs to Enhance This Combo

What we can't see in this June view is all of the bulbs that are in this bed. This spring display includes *Erythronium* 'Pagoda', *Scilla siberica* 'Alba', tulip 'Sweetheart', blue hyacinths around the dormant hostas, and of course, lots of narcissus!

### Stinking hellebore
*Helleborus foetidus*

The deep green, palmlike leaves of the stinking hellebore are perfect for massing in the dappled shade of trees. Don't let the name scare you; stinking hellebore is stinky only when its leaves are crushed. The bell-shaped flowers, often *pleasantly* scented and sometimes outlined with red margins, appear in midwinter to midspring. Likes neutral to alkaline soil. Hardy to Zone 6. 32" tall × 18" wide.

### Golden creeping Jenny
*Lysimachia nummularia* 'Aurea'

Low, gold, and rampant, creeping Jenny's tiny, heart-shaped leaves are attractive creeping over the edges of walls or, as it is used here, as a carpet for blue grasses to pop out of. In the summer, golden creeping Jenny complements its yellow foliage with cup-shaped, bright yellow flowers. Be careful, though — since its stems root as they grow, so once you have it, you have it for good! Hardy to Zone 4. 2" tall × indefinite width.

### 'Silk Tassel' sedge
*Carex morrowii* 'Silk Tassel'

Grown for its very fine-textured blades, 'Silk Tassel' sedge looks indeed a little like the hair of the earth. In this scene, the blue coloration of the blades is brought out by the underplanting of golden creeping Jenny. Occasionally, 'Silk Tassel' will revert to a green form, as one plant in this arrangement has done. 'Silk Tassel' sedge likes fertile, moist, well-drained soil in sun or part shade. Hardy to Zone 5. 12" tall × 24" wide.

### Autumn fern
*Dryopteris erythrosora*

Providing a welcome, upright splash of red, this Japanese import provides dramatic texture to this combo. Known for its prominent red *sori* (fish eye–like bumps on the underside of the fronds that produce spores), the new fronds of autumn fern are coppery red. Great for protected, moist beds. Hardy to Zone 5. 24" tall × 15" wide.

### 'Yellow River' Hosta
*Hosta* 'Yellow River'

This fairly upright hosta has yellow margins and pale lavender flower spikes. Here, it echoes the vertical shape of the adjacent autumn fern. Hardy to Zone 3. 22" tall × 36" wide.

### Yellow toad lily
*Tricyrtis macranthopsis*

This draping toad lily helps hide what would be bare ground beneath the hosta. Its pendant, bell-shaped flowers are bright yellow. When it comes to toad lilies, beware of slugs. As Janet Draper remarks, "I don't normally have a slug problem, but they find these flowers rather tasty. I'm thinking that the plant would be shown off better if it could cascade over the wall entirely — then the sluggos couldn't get to it." Draper also recommends keeping the toad lily wet. "It needs adequate moisture, or the foliage looks nasty, which detracts from the really cool golden flowers." Hardy to Zone 8. 16"–32" tall × 12" wide.

# GRINDING OUT A COFFEE-COLORED COMBO

Part of what makes this garden vignette in front of an antique mill-stone so intriguing is designer Inta Krombolz's innovative use of the color brown. A monochromatic color scheme is unusual, but one featuring mocha-colored plants is almost unheard of. Krombolz uses her signature 'Helmond Pillar' Japanese barberries as exclamation points to contrast with the softer look of the light brown leatherleaf sedge. The effect of the whole collection is an unusually subtle use of foliage and form that appears as tasty as a well-crafted latte.

*A monochromatic color scheme of mocha-colored plants is almost unheard of.*

### 'Helmond Pillar' Japanese barberry
*Berberis thunbergii* 'Helmond Pillar'
This unique barberry makes an excellent vertical accent, especially when its color is echoed in surrounding plants, as it is here. Hardy to Zone 4. 4'–5' tall × 1'–2' wide.

### Leatherleaf sedge
*Carex buchananii*
This densely evergreen (or should it be called evertawny?) grass from New Zealand has a pleasing, arching habit and russet-colored foliage. Inta Krombolz recommends planting it in a mix with a lot of grit, as it likes fast drainage. Hardy to Zone 6. 20"–30" tall × 36" wide.

### 'Midnight Wine' weigela
*Weigela florida* 'Midnight Wine'
Growing between the leatherleaf sedge, 'Midnight Wine' is the perfect color complement for this combinaton. It's a dwarf, low-rounded shrub with reddish pink blooms. Although some descriptions list its foliage color as purple, as you can see here, it tends toward a brown-toned red. Hardy to Zone 4. 1.5'–2' tall × 1.5'–2' wide.

### Magic Carpet spirea
*Spiraea japonica* 'Walbuma' (Magic Carpet)
This multihued dwarf shrub has green-gold foliage with red leaf tips. Early spring flowers are deep pink-purple and cover the plant over a long season. In autumn, foliage changes to russet tones. Low spreading habit. Full sun. Hardy to Zone 3. 18" tall × 2' wide.

*designer tips*

## Use Monofilament to Shape Fastigiate Growers

To keep your *fastigiate* (narrow, pointed) plants in tidy columns, Inta Krombolz suggests getting out your tackle box and wrapping monofilament fishing line around your columnar plants to keep them in tight form. The fishing line is virtually invisible and lends a sculptural quality to plants like 'Helmond Pillar' Japanese barberry.

# Prairie Classics

When you think of prairie plantings, you might picture vast, grassy meadows bejeweled with milkweeds and coneflowers — something much too expansive to consider for a suburban front yard. If you look closer, though, you'll see that prairie planting design is easily applied to even small home gardens. The trick is to dial down your focus to a smaller group of plants — like the three prairie classics featured here in this Neil Diboll design in a Wisconsin front yard. As Diboll comments, "There is no archetypal prairie model but using [clumping ornamental] grasses and flowers together is classic prairie style." Diboll begins his design process by matching the plants to the soil conditions. Here, he establishes clumps of silvery little bluestem around purple coneflower with a white lacy backdrop of wild quinine — a planting that could be used in many sunny situations in town and country.

*Grasses and flowers together is classic prairie style.*

### designer tips

## Root Power

Because about 70 percent of the average prairie plant is composed of roots, this group of plants is peerless in its ability to store nutrients and moisture below ground. The root systems of prairie plants facilitate their long-term survival; native prairie plants live not for years, but for decades. One advantage of combining grasses and flowers is that their roots occupy different zones in the soil — something Neil Diboll calls "the partitioning of the root environment." What that means for gardeners is that the grasses, plants like little bluestem, have roots in the top two to four feet of soil. Many of the flowering perennials, like the wild quinine, may root as deep as 8 or 10 feet! Roots this extensive take more than one or two seasons to mature, so be patient, and as you look at your plants, remember that most of them is underground.

### Purple coneflower
*Echinacea purpurea*

Likely the most popular native perennial in America, purple coneflower's hardiness, beguiling orange-green eyes, and pink rays are hard to resist. Although it seems that every plant breeder in the country has been tinkering with purple coneflower in hopes of producing an unusual hybrid, the good old straight species has a lot going for it. Blooming July through September, it seems to be visited by entire flocks of butterflies, and hummingbirds are known to visit the flowers as well. Long-lived and easy to grow, it is a good way to cut your teeth on prairie plants. Likes average garden soil and even tolerates clay. Full sun to part shade. Hardy to Zone 4. 3'–4' tall × 1' wide.

### Little bluestem
*Schizachyrium scoparium*

One of the most-loved prairie grasses, little bluestem is blue-green in summer and crimson in fall, when it sends up fluffy, silver seed heads. Little bluestem is a great companion for almost any flowering prairie perennial that will grow in well-drained soils. Prefers sandy to average soils and full sun. Hardy to Zone 4. 2'–3' tall × 1' wide.

### Wild quinine
*Parthenium integrifolium*

Wild quinine is notable for its sizable, umbel-shaped, pure white flowers that bloom over a long season, from June clear through September. This gardenworthy prairie native was once considered rare and unusual but is now available in the trade. It has interesting serrated leaves and is resistant to, as Diboll puts it, "just about every bug, disease, and weather problem there is." This long-lived plant develops a strong taproot (in some cases up to eight feet deep). Here, it mingles nicely behind purple coneflower like a native and better-behaved Queen Anne's lace (*Daucus carota*). Hardy to Zone 4. 3'–5' tall × 12" wide.

# SIBERIAN SAVANNA

Garden designers often encourage their clients to limit the number of species in their gardens in order to turn out a bolder, more coherent design. Sometimes the number of plant species needed is only two. In this case, Russian sage and Siberian graybeard are more than up to the task. The Russian sage is planted en masse like a blue canvas for the sizable green mounds of Siberian graybeard. Although this planting is sited on a slope in the Chicago Botanic Gardens, gardeners with modernist tastes and a little chutzpah could replace an entire front lawn with a simple, waist-high meadow of blue and green.

## designer tips

### Make Your Garden Relaxed, Reduce Your Chemical Use

The landscape design firm Oehme, van Sweden Associates uses tough perennial plants like Russian sage combined with ornamental grasses to reduce the use of fertilizers and excessive irrigation in American gardens. This is in keeping with their design philosophy for what they call "New American Garden" style, an alternative to typical gardens that is more relaxed and requires no deadheading or pesticides.

**Russian sage**
*Perovskia atriplicifolia*
A workhorse in the hot, dry garden, the lavender-like blooms of Russian sage are a welcome late-summer and fall treat. The interesting, white stems and deeply cut leaves add interest to the plant, even when it's out of bloom. Tolerates heat and poor, alkaline soils. Hardy to Zone 5. 4' tall × 3' wide.

**Siberian graybeard**
*Spodiopogon sibiricus*
Siberian graybeard is a bamboo-like clumping grass with unusual blades that splay open in a horizontal fashion. In late summer, the leaves turn wine colored, and foot-long, feathery, purple panicles float over the plant. Give full sun to part shade with regular watering. Hardy to Zone 5. 4' tall × 3'–3.5' wide.

*A simple, waist-high meadow of blue and green*

# Riot around Rocky Top

This painterly planting demonstrates just how thoroughly Piet Oudolf has deconstructed traditional formal borders, transforming planting beds into crazy quilts of naturalistic yet intentional patterns. This combination is a riot of textures and forms; from the misty love grass to upright alliums, the planting evokes nature and formal horticulture simultaneously. Like coastal fog, love grass creeps into the mixture, looking as though it might overtake the larger perennials — that is, until it runs hard up against the upright allium, which definitely holds its own in this planting.

## designer tips

### Marry Wild Natives with Highly Bred Cultivars

Almost everyone loves a meadow of wildflowers, but trying to incorporate native plants into a tidy front garden is quite another task. Piet Oudolf is a master at marrying wild and domesticated plants, and this cluster clearly shows that mixing wildish plants such as 'Rocky Top' coneflower and purple love grass with sophisticates like 'Matrona' sedum and ornamental onion is one of the best ways to have your garden two ways: wild *and* tame.

### Purple love grass
*Eragrostis spectabilis*
The airy seed heads of purple love grass seem to roll into this combination like fog off the nearby Hudson River. Excellent for naturalistic plantings, this native prefers sandy soil. The spikelets and flowers begin pink-purple and gradually turn a rusty brown. After maturity, the plant has a curious habit: its dried inflorescence will often break free and roll like a tumbleweed into your neighbor's yard or the next county. Although it is native to much of the United States, in some areas it can be aggressive and invasive. Hardy to Zone 6. 18"–24" tall × 18"–24" wide.

### 'Rocky Top' coneflower
*Echinacea tennesseensis* 'Rocky Top'
An endangered southeastern native, 'Rocky Top' is a compact coneflower whose pink rays track the sun. It will take full sun or partial shade. Hardy to Zone 4. 24"–36" tall × 12" wide.

### Ornamental onion
*Allium stipitatum*
Up against the edge of the sprawling, tawny, love grass seed head, this ornamental onion does the green heavy lifting here. With its deep green, strappy leaves and upright habit, it brings some civility to the more unruly plants around it, producing tightly arranged, drumstick-shaped, white umbels. Hardy to Zone 4. 2–4' tall × 12" wide.

### 'Matrona' sedum
*Sedum* 'Matrona'
This sedum hybrid from Germany (a seedling from a cross of 'Atropurpureum' and 'Autumn Joy') has taken the garden design world by storm. In 1998, 'Matrona' won the Outstanding Perennial Award from the International Hardy Plant Union. Here it makes an excellent, well-rounded — even matronly — companion to the more upright alliums and coneflowers surrounding it. Hardy to Zone 3. 30" tall × 12"–24" wide.

*A riot of textures and forms; from the misty love grass to upright alliums*

# LITTLE BUNNY JEWEL BOX BED

Perhaps because small plants always seem to be in short supply, people are captivated with dwarf or compact cultivars. This Scott Rothenberger–designed corner planting bed is a great example of how different textures and colors, especially when they are repeated, produce a rich tapestry in a layout that consists of only three plants. Two of the plants — 'Little Bunny' fountain grass and 'Fens Ruby' spurge — are miniature and create a jewel box look when planted together.

*Different textures and colors create a rich tapestry.*

**'Issai' beautyberry**
*Callicarpa dichotoma* 'Issai'
Known for its shiny, violet fruit clustered on long, arching stems, beautyberry is used here to arch over the plants below. 'Issai', is a smaller cultivar that bears heavy berries at an early age. Hardy to Zone 5. 2'–4' tall × 3'–5' wide.

**'Little Bunny' fountain grass**
*Pennisetum alopecuroides* 'Little Bunny'
This little fountain grass is so named because its fluffy seed heads resemble bunny tails. Its compact size and round form do much to recommend it to gardeners. Hardy to Zone 6. 10"–12" tall × 10"–12" wide.

**'Fens Ruby' spurge**
*Euphorbia cyparissias* 'Fens Ruby'
Its small size and texture resembling blue spruce needles make 'Fens Ruby' a winner for filling in between grasses. The name 'Fens Ruby' seems to be somewhat of a misnomer, because neither its leaves nor its flowers are a deep shade of red. Rather, it sports the more typical blue-gray euphorbia leaves with yellow-green flowers. In early spring, its new growth is a sort of pink color. In some climates, 'Fens Ruby' can spread aggressively and become invasive. Hardy to Zone 4. 8" tall × indefinite width.

## designer tips

### Arch-Over Plants
Plants like beautyberry that arch over their neighbors without shading them out or competing with them can be great assets. Other plants with long, arching stems to consider are 'Lady Banks' rose (*Rosa banksiae*) and silver fountain butterfly bush (*Buddleia alternifolia* 'Argentea').

# Switchgrass and Shakespeare's Sisters

Sometimes inspiring design ideas result from breaking the rules. In this arrangement, Duncan Brine nudges a plant that typically prefers moist conditions, 'Desdemona' golden groundsel, into an area that is a little drier and sunnier than would usually be recommended. In Brine's concoction, the 'Desdemona' seedling tolerates more sun and drier soil than most groundsels, which Brine says "wilt like picked lettuce in the afternoon sun." The resulting assemblage is captivating. The fine linear leaves of the grass contrast well with the large, round leaves of 'Desdemona'. The low branch of the 'Royal Purple' smoke tree ties in with the bold, red veination seen on the backside of the generous groundsel leaf. In the foreground, the silvery lamb's ears provides a cool, soft transition to the bolder foliage plants behind.

designer tips

## Make Basins for Moisture-Loving Plants

Because plants like groundsel like it on the wet side, one way to incorporate them into plantings with companion plants that like it on the dry side is to plant them in lower basins. The basins don't have to look like an archaeological dig; a shallow subtle depression is often all that's needed for a moisture-loving plant to get a little extra water and thrive.

### 'Desdemona' golden groundsel
*Ligularia dentata 'Desdemona'*
The main attraction of 'Desdemona' is its large, round, green-brown — almost chocolate-colored — leaves, which have distinctive purple-red veins on their undersides. Summer through early autumn, golden groundsel produces sizable stalks topped with yellow daisylike flowers. It's an unusually colored plant that likes reliably moist soil and some protection from the afternoon sun. Hardy to Zone 4. 3' tall × 3' wide.

### Switchgrass
*Panicum virgatum*
Switchgrass is so vigorous, it's being evaluated as a possible corn-replacement in ethanol production. Broad, mid-green leaves, great size, and a mostly upright habit define this easy and carefree grass. Large purple-green seed spikelets are produced in early autumn. In this combination, switchgrass serves as a vertical accent to the surrounding plants with more rounded leaves. Zone 5. 3' tall × 30" wide.

### 'Big Ears' lamb's ears
*Stachys byzantina 'Big Ears'*
This ideal edging plant is the perfect foreground plant in this combination. Because lamb's ears needs good drainage, Brine situates the plant higher than groundsel, which appreciates the extra water. 'Big Ears', synonymous with the cultivar 'Helene von Stein', is more tolerant of high humidity and less prone to summer dieback than regular lamb's ears. Hardy to Zone 4. 10" tall × 24" wide.

### 'Royal Purple' smoke tree
*Cotinus coggygria 'Royal Purple'*
Although only one low branch of this plant creeps into the photo, it provides a dash of red-purple that is the perfect mediator between 'Big Ears' and 'Desdemona'. Hardy to Zone 5. 15' tall × 15' wide.

*The fine linear leaves of the grass contrast well with the large, round leaves of 'Desdemona'.*

# ANNUAL
# *Acquaintances*

If annuals, plants that go through their entire life cycle in one year, had a credo, it might be something like "Grow fast, flower hard, and die young." Not surprisingly, annuals bring color and excitement to gardens. The annuals in this chapter may not be what you think of when you picture annuals. By design, we are short on marigolds and petunias. There's nothing wrong with those flowers; they simply are so ubiquitous that garden designers seem to avoid them like the plague. I am reminded of something the late great gardening columnist for the *Washington Post*, Henry Mitchell, wrote: "A fellow reproaches me for mentioning too many plants he's never heard of and not enough of the ones he has. Marigold, marigold, marigold. So much for that."

Although designers and horticulturists are not planting many marigolds and petunias these days, they are using lots of interesting annual flowering plants, and many won't design a garden without them. They use annuals as little bursts of color mixed into larger gardens — seasonal splashes that can escape heat, drought, or cold by going dormant. Annuals can be used to fill in the gaps between perennials, grasses, and woody plants, and can be left to reseed for a naturalistic effect. It's safe to say that designers tend to use annuals as flourishes, rather than mainstays — letting woody plants, grasses, accents, and perennials do more of the heavy lifting.

This is not to say that annuals aren't important. In the plantings in this chapter, annual flowers enliven, brighten, and fill in like no other plants can. In the following section on annual combinations, you'll find a blissfully textured, white garden ensemble as well as simple combinations, like a single clump of Shirley poppies whose pink flowers appear like a painter's flourish against a sage green background. Growing annuals from seed is all about relinquishing some control in the garden — letting seeds find their niches and eagerly awaiting the results. It can be cheap and offers a little instant gratification that will make it a little easier to wait for perennials and shrubs to mature.

Sometimes red is all you need — in this case, zinnias (*Zinnia*) and globe amaranth (*Gomphrena globosa*).

# Pink Saucers
## above
## Sea Foam

It's no wonder that landscape
painters are so fond of the
Shirley poppy as a subject; its
double flower petals are hot
pink at the edges and fade to
white near the flower's eye
— as if their color had been
applied using skilled brush-
strokes. Panayoti Kelaidis is
able to leverage the pink and
white of the Shirley flowers
by providing a fine-textured,
silver, mat background of
'Sea Foam' sage. The suc-
cess of this combination is
its Zen-like simplicity, which
is expressed in the limited
color palette of hot pink, silver, and green. Although the
planting is simple, Kelaidis
includes other plant treasures
that extend seasonal interest, such as a low-growing
Veronica, Mexican feather
grass, and scarlet bugler.

*A Zen-like palette expressed in hot pink, silver, and green*

## Shirley poppy
*Papaver × rhoeas*

Shirley poppies are a strain of Flander's poppy bred for desirable garden characteristics in Shirley, England, in the late nineteenth century. Instead of just the basic red and black of the Flander's poppy, Shirley poppies are available in crimson, rose, pink, salmon, cream, and white, as well as variations including white flowers tipped with peach or hot pink tipped with white. Although most Shirley poppies are double-flowered, single varieties as well as semidoubles and crinkled and ruffled versions are available. Like Flander's poppy, Shirley poppy is an annual that is almost always grown from seed. In the southern regions of the United States, it's sown in fall; in northern regions, in early spring. Sow seeds on the surface and allow 10 to 30 days for germination. Annual. 12"–18" tall × 12"–15" wide.

## Curlicue artemisia
*Artemisia versicolor 'Seafoam'*

Introduced to the United States from England by Lauren Springer Ogden, 'Seafoam' deserves a place in more gardens. Low, silver, and very aromatic, curlicue artemisia is known for its "foamy," curling leaves. It adds a soft lacy contrast to surrounding plants that are more stiff, upright, and architectural. Much more compact than 'Powis Castle' and seemingly just as vigorous. Hardy to Zone 4. 8" tall × 24" wide.

## Turkish wedgeleaf veronica
*Veronica cuneifolia*

A squat, mat-forming veronica with exceptional drought tolerance and medium blue flowers in spring. Provide well-drained soil. Hardy to Zone 3. 3" tall × 12" wide.

## Scarlet bugler penstemon
*Penstemon barbatus*

Growing next to the Shirley poppy, the burgundy stems and red, tubular flowers also contrast nicely with the curlicue artemisia and, like the Shirley poppy, reseed readily. Slender, gray-green leaves extend from the stems at 90-degree angles. Provide well-drained soil. Hardy to Zone 4. 1' (2' flower spike) tall × 1' wide .

## Mexican feather grass
*Nassella tenuissima*

As John Greenlee says, Mexican feather grass is "the blonde of grasses." Its fine, almost delicate texture belies its true tough-as-nails nature. In the city of Santa Fe, Mexican feather grass is ubiquitous and seems to have become the self-appointed street-median grass of the city. This speaks to its prodigious reseeding habit, which should not be underestimated. The good news is that Mexican feather grass seedlings are shallow rooted and easily pulled out. Hardy to Zone 5. 2' × 2' wide.

---

### designer tips

## For Seasonal Interest, Bring in a Reserve Player

When you have a grouping that relies, as this combination does, on one flashy plant (in this case the Shirley poppy) with relatively brief bloom season, you can have a back-up player ready to take its place. In this case, just as the Shirley poppy is done blooming, the scarlet bugler penstemon will display its red flowers on tall stalks, looking every bit as fetching as the Shirley poppy against the background of curlicue sage.

# CANNA BANANA REPUBLIC

Behind a low 'Green Mountain' boxwood hedge, Chanticleer horticulturist Dan Benarcik works some voo-doo subtropical plant magic, keying off the color orange. "I began with the red-range flowering 'Australia' canna and combined it with the bright, rust-colored 'Rustic Orange' coleus. From there I added large-leafed tropicals to round out the planting." The result, brimming with bananas, cannas, and angel's trumpet, is its own little banana republic.

*Dan Benarcik works some subtropical voodoo magic.*

### 'Maurelii' Abyssinian banana
*Ensete ventricosum* 'Maurelii'
The canoe paddle–shaped leaves of the banana-like plant hang over this planting like a trio of parasols. The dark red color of the midribs and leaf margins produces a synergy with the burgundy-black canna foliage. Hardy to Zone 10. (In colder regions 'Maurelii' is grown in a temperate green-house, then planted out in summer for tropical effects.) 20' tall × 15' wide.

### 'Australia' canna lily
*Canna* 'Australia'
This New Zealand native, with leaves so shiny and burgundy-black that they appear shellacked, is a very unusual canna. There are many cultivars with red or striped foliage, but none quite so dark and lusty as 'Australia'. Hardy to Zone 7. 60" tall × 24" wide.

### 'Cypress Gardens' angel's trumpet
*Brugmansia* 'Cypress Gardens'
In addition to its startling, hanging, trumpet-shaped flowers, the wide leaves of angel's trumpet have appeal on their own. 'Cypress Gardens' is known for its almost pure white, large blossoms with distinctly upturned petal edges. As with all angel's trumpets, all parts of this tomato-family plant are poisonous. Although Dan Benarcik is a fan of plants in the *Brugmansia* genus, 'Cypress Gardens' has been a disappointment for him. Instead, he recommends 'Snowbank' angel's trumpet (*Brugmansia* 'Snowbank') as a replacement. Both 'Cypress Gardens' and 'Snowbank' are hardy to Zone 8. 60" tall × 36" wide.

### 'Rustic Orange' coleus
*Solenostemon* 'Rustic Orange'
When surrounded by burgundy and green, this coppery coleus electrifies borders. Its leaves emerge muted red, turning bright rust with maturity. Hardy to Zone 11; grown as an annual or overwintered in colder zones. 12"–18" tall × 15" wide.

### 'Tortile' croton
*Codiaeum* 'Tortile'
This croton is a compact and bushy plant, with spirally twisting, thick, waxy leaves that begin bright yellow and turn orange and red with green veins as they mature. It's usually grown as a houseplant but is adaptable to outdoor culture as well. Hardy to Zone 13; grown as an annual or overwintered in colder zones. 3' tall × 3' wide.

---

*designer tips*

## Overwintering Angel's Trumpet

There are two ways to get your angel's trumpet through the winter — in a greenhouse or bright window or in a dormant state. In a greenhouse or in a bright, south-facing window, angel's trumpet can be kept growing all winter. Lacking these conditions, cut back the angel's trumpet hard, leaving several inches of stem above the soil level. Store it in a frost-free location and bring it back out after chance of frost has passed.

# TRAFFIC TRIANGLE TANGO

Twenty-five years after petitioning the city and getting permission to plant the triangular-shaped traffic island in front of her home, Mary Lou Gross is still creating slam-on-the-brakes beauty in her Wilmington, Delaware, median bed. In fact, you are required by law to hit the brakes because of stop signs that sit in the planting bed itself. "I really wanted this [planting bed] because my small urban backyard is too shady and I wanted a place to grow a lot of sun-loving plants, many of them annuals." The bed, not cluttered by trees, shrubs, or other shade producers, is perfect for sun lovers. The triangle begins blooming in spring with red and yellow tulips and daffodils, followed by irises and larkspur. As pictured here, in late-summer form, the bed is amok with chartreuse sweet potato vine interspersed with 'Little Spire' Russian sage, 'Viette's Little Suzy' dwarf black-eyed Susan, and a wisp of tall verbena.

*designer tips*

## Cool Down the Hot Mix

Beds that are all hot colors might not leave a serene spot for your eyes to rest. If you've got a hot bed, you may need to balance out all the oranges, reds, and golds with some peeps from the cool side of the color wheel. Like a club DJ easing sweaty, worked-up teens into a slow song after a pulsing techno tune, Mary Lou Gross cools down the golds and chartreuses in her plantings "by adding in purples like *Salvia farinacea* 'Victoria Blue', *Perovskia atriplicifolia* 'Little Spire', and *Verbena bonariensis*."

### 'Margarita' sweet potato vine
*Ipomoea batatas* 'Margarita'

'Margarita' is a plant that is not afraid of warm or even downright hot colors, as Mary Lou Gross comments: "In the garden I plant it with hot-colored annuals like zinnas in scarlet, yellow, or orange colors; gaillardia (blanket flower) in red, yellow, or orange colors; and golden rudbeckia." One of the chartreuse-leafed selections of sweet potato vine, 'Margarita' is great for a quick, electric-green ground cover. You can almost watch sweet potato grow from its carbohydrate-packed tuber in warm weather. It takes sun to part sun, a moderate amount of water, and average soil. It also comes in a near-black form called 'Blackie'. Hardy to Zone 11; grown as an annual almost everywhere. 6" tall × 10'–20' wide.

### 'Little Spire' Russian sage
*Perovskia atriplicifolia* 'Little Spire'

A tough, low-maintenance perennial that takes full sun, 'Little Spire' has violet-blue flowers, and it blooms from June to frost. It's an open, airy plant that mixes well with shorter, denser companions. A compact version of the common and much-used Russian sage, 'Little Spire' grows only 24 inches tall and wide, whereas the straight species can reach 3 to 4 feet. Hardy to Zone 4. 2' tall × 2' wide.

### 'Viette's Little Suzy' dwarf black-eyed Susan
*Rudbeckia fulgida* 'Viette's Little Suzy'

Who can resist a plant that sounds as if it were named after a French madam's miniature poodle? This dwarf cultivar, 'Viette's Little Suzy', looks like *Rudbeckia hirta,* except it's a little lighter in gold color and is shorter. Grow in moderately fertile but well-drained soil in full sun or partial shade. It is a low-maintenance plant that flowers from midsummer to frost. 'Viette's Little Suzy' plays well with other hot colors and with purples in the garden. Hardy to Zone 3. 12–18" × 9"–12" wide.

*Balance the gold with some peeps from the cool side of the color wheel.*

# THE CALL OF ANGEL'S TRUMPETS

When you place a plant as glorious as 'Snowbank' angel's trumpet right in the middle of a bed, all of the other surrounding plants must respond to it. When I first saw this substantial, variegated beauty in Nancy Ondra's garden, I exclaimed in delight. Then I looked around it and noticed that Nancy had nudged a portly 'Redbor' kale up against it, along with warm-season grasses, a veronica, and a white globe amaranth. The color scheme — green, white, blue, with a dash of purple veination in the kale — both soothes and stimulates.

*Variegated foliage is invaluable for adding all-season interest.*

### 'Snowbank' angel's trumpet
*Brugmansia* 'Snowbank'

Plantsman Tony Avent describes 'Snowbank' as one of those plants that is so beautiful it'll make you "fall to your knees and weep." Its huge leaves are variegated in tricolor splotches of cream and greens that resemble pixilated camouflage. Really, the foliage is enough to thrill with this plant, but the audacious, fragrant, apricot-colored flowers are one more point of doctrine with which to convert the disbeliever. Zone 7. 5' tall × 4'–5' wide.

### 'Redbor' kale
*Brassica oleracea* 'Redbor'

Sidled up to the 'Snowbank' angel's trumpet, 'Redbor' kale, with its purple-red ruffles, provides welcome contrast to the other green, cream, and white colors in the planting. In warm, southerly zones, 'Redbor' is a winter grower, providing color from October through April. In more northerly zones, it's planted in late spring. The red color intensifies with cold weather and the leaves are tender and sweet. It's another great example, in the cottage garden tradition, of a vegetable with a future in the ornamental garden. Grow as an annual. 18" tall × 12"–18" wide.

### Mexican feather grass
*Nassella tenuissima*

Hardly anyone can resist the fine, hairlike texture and chartreuse color of Mexican feather grass, which here serves to hide the lower bare stalk of the 'Snowbank' angel's trumpet. Mexican feather grass, whose other common name, "ponytail grass," alludes to the clump of fine seed heads that form at its top, is a ready reseeder, but one whose seedlings are easily yanked up. Hardy to Zone 5. 2' tall × 2' wide.

### 'Buddy White' globe amaranth
*Gomphrena globosa* 'Buddy White'

Originally a Central American tropical plant, globe amaranth has been bred to provide good color display on compact plants. An example of this breeding is found in 'Buddy White'. A subdued cousin to the hugely popular 'Strawberry Fields' cultivar, 'Buddy White' is compact, sending up multitudes of round-headed, drumsticklike flowers. Annual. 6" tall × 6" wide.

### 'Goodness Grows' speedwell
*Veronica* 'Goodness Grows'

The little prostrate speedwell works so well in this planting because it stays low and weaves its way through the verbena and variegated St. Augustine grass, adding little, cool purple-blue spikelets to the white and green. Hardy to Zone 3. 12" tall × 14" wide.

# BESIDE GRANITE STEPS

When Joe Henderson designed this hillside planting beside wide, granite steps ascending to an arbor-covered patio, he took the advice of the late Christopher Lloyd. "I tried to maximize the space and make it work as much and as long as possible." A statuesque cardoon sits at the center of the bed surrounded by rose-purple and electric orange flowers, while tall 'Northwind' switchgrass presides over the other plants from the edge of the stairs. "This is a gravel garden. I only water the plants to get them started and thereafter only when absolutely necessary." In order to create good growing conditions for his gravel garden, Henderson amends the soil with sand and small river jack, which is the size of pea gravel. "I was trying an idea from Beth Chatto's dry garden here at Chanticleer. She does not irrigate and gets less than 20 inches of rain a year and her stuff does fine," says Henderson.

*A statuesque cardoon,
surrounded by rose-purple
and electric orange*

## Cardoon
*Cynara cardunculus*
This rough and tumble artichoke relative is impossible to ignore. Its silver foliage and rosette form make it the centerpiece of this planting. Although native to Morocco and the Mediterranean, cardoon will grow in temperate climates and, according to Henderson, is not aggressive in northern gardens. Summer through fall, purple, thistle-shaped seed heads rise from the silver foliage. The midribs of its leaves are edible; look a lot like pale, pumped-up celery; and are often used in Italian recipes (see Eat Your Landscape). In warmer climates, globe artichoke (*Cynara scolymus*) is a good substitute. Hardy to Zone 7. 6'–8' tall × 4' wide.

## 'Bright Lights' cosmos
*Cosmos sulphureus* 'Bright Lights'
The glowing orange flowers of 'Bright Lights' set it apart from the white and pink shades often found in grandmothers' gardens. This Mexican native is vigorous and prolific; as Joe Henderson remarks, "There are always a lot of volunteers to edit." 'Bright Lights' is a very good butterfly attractor, and its fine foliage and long, leaning flower stems further define this plant as a barely tamed wild one. Annual. 3'–6' tall × 18" wide.

## Texas hummingbird mint
*Agastache cana*
This is the lofty, pink, hummingbird attractor of the display. Its highly fragrant leaves smell a little like bubble gum — hence its nickname, "double-bubble mint." This plant is native to west Texas and New Mexico but is right at home in the amended sandy soil at Chanticleer. Although its slender stems are a nod to the 'Bright Lights' cosmos around it, its rose-purple flowers are on the other side of the color wheel from the orange of 'Bright Lights'. Hardy to Zone 6. 16"–24" tall × 18" wide.

## 'Northwind' switchgrass
*Panicum virgatum* 'Northwind'
Perhaps more than any plant in this bunch, 'Northwind' switchgrass visually marries the plant material to the garden. That is, the strongly upright form of the switchgrass suggests the vertical design of the thronelike garden chairs beneath the arbor in the background. 'Northwind' has olive green foliage and lacy, open, bloom spikes. Like 'Bright Lights' cosmos, Joe Henderson explains that 'Northwind' is a "plant that really sets a lot of seeds into the garden." Hardy to Zone 4. 60" tall × 18" wide.

## designer tips

### Eat Your Landscape
We often consider ornamental gardens one thing and vegetable gardens quite another; this combination demonstrates that ornamental and culinary plants can be mixed successfully — some vegetables are highly ornamental and some ornamental plants are delectably edible. As Joe Henderson says about cardoon, "I find it in the Italian market in downtown Philadelphia, where they cook it in milk to reduce its bitterness, and then bake it with Ementhaler cheese. It is quite tasty." Grow cardoon as a cool-season veggie for best flavor. In warmer weather, the normally sweet flavor can become bitter.

If you're looking for a garden with round foliage and yellow speckles, this Brandon Tyson design will do just fine. The big circular leaves of leopard plant (*Farfugium japonicum*) echo the shape of the leaves of the *Nasturtium* 'Peach Melba', while a yellow tassel of millet grass (*Millium effusum* 'Aureum') emerges from between the two.

# Electric Blanket Hillside

A gentle slope with a view is the perfect place for a durable ground cover blanket comprising two tough perennials and one surprising annual. The annual, 'Marine' heliotrope, makes the planting an electric blanket, with its deep blue flowers and deep green leaves popping through the gray foliage of 'Big Ears' lamb's ears. Because the three plants used here are low growers, the plants take on the role of a highly textured quilt, providing erosion control and visual beauty simultaneously. This combination at Chicago Botanic Gardens was designed by Lisa Delplace of Oehme, van Sweden & Associates, and although the space may be somewhat larger than what most home gardeners have to work with, its design is applicable on a residential scale.

## designer tips

### Working with Views

Homeowners with views are often scared to plant anything, especially trees, that might impinge on their vistas. A better approach might be to think about framing a view or hiding and then revealing it through the use of plants. In this example, the low plantings are arresting because 300 crab apples are planted around the basin to conceal and, by their absence, reveal a vantage point. When you emerge from a tunnel of crab apples into a vast expanse of low silver and blue ground covers with water in the background, this technique is breathtaking.

*A highly textured quilt, providing erosion control and visual beauty*

**'Marine' heliotrope**
*Heliotropium arborescens* 'Marine'
The deep blue, highly fragrant, vanilla-scented flowers of 'Marine' heliotrope attract both humans and butterflies. The deep purple is especially effective when intermingled with silver foliage plants, as shown here. Full sun to part shade. Annual. 24" tall × 12" wide.

**'Big Ears' lamb's ears**
*Stachys byzantina* 'Big Ears'
'Big Ears' is a workhorse, and its soft leaves help mediate between the pink of coneflower and yellow of the daylilies. The cultivar 'Big Ears' is synonymous with the cultivar 'Helene von Stein' and is more tolerant of high humidity and less prone to summer dieback than regular lamb's ears. Hardy to Zone 4. 10" tall × 24" wide.

**'Six Hills Giant' catmint**
*Nepeta* 'Six Hills Giant'
The gray-green catmint is a fine foil for just about any color, and, as a bonus, its odor repels deer. The catmint also blooms for about a month and reblooms after being cut back. Its foliage lasts well into December, and it attracts bees, beneficial insects, butterflies, and hummingbirds, as well as hummingbird moths. Hardy to Zone 3. 36" tall × 24" wide.

# AN ANNUAL WHITEOUT

Showy, pristine, and silver, this combo at Longwood Gardens highlights what can be done with annuals planted en masse. A filigree carpet of 'Silver Queen' dusty miller, a stripe of 'Brookside Snowball' dahlia, and a snippet of angel wings caladium make up the foreground of this snowstorm of a planting. In the background, the spent flowers of Japanese clethra add interesting whiskey-colored texture.

### 'Silver Queen' dusty miller

*Senecio cineraria* 'Silver Queen'

'Silver Queen' is much used in annual plantings, where it's combined with other, usually brightly colored, summer annuals, but seeing it on its own, in a mass of velvety silver, seems to be a more interesting use for dusty miller. This cultivar is a more compact grower than garden-variety dusty miller. Hardy to Zone 8; grown as an annual in most climates. 8" tall × 12"–24" wide.

### 'Candidum' angel wings caladium

*Caladium* 'Candidum'

A South American tropical, angel wings offer white leaves with green veins that mirror the color of 'Morning Light' maiden grass and provide a nice, bold, foliage contrast with the dusty miller growing up against it. Grown from a tuber, it likes hot weather and even soil moisture. Hardy to Zone 15; annual almost everywhere (see Save Your Tuberous Tropical Annuals for overwintering advice). 24" tall × 24" wide.

### 'Morning Light' maiden grass

*Miscanthus sinensis* 'Morning Light'

The 'Morning Light' maiden grass right in the center of this photo emerges from a silver sea of dusty miller. This white-striped, variegated grass produces coppery, tassel-like flower stalks that turn wheat colored in winter and persist for good winter interest. It's a great wild-looking accent to break up more formal plantings. Hardy to Zone 5. 4'–6' tall × 2.5'–4' wide.

### 'Brookside Snowball' dahlia

*Dahlia* 'Brookside Snowball'

This small-flowered ball dahlia makes a nice strip of white and green between the dusty miller and the Japanese clethra. Dahlias like rich, fertile, moist soil and full sun. Hardy to Zone 9; elsewhere, store the tubers for winter. 2'–4' tall × 2'–4' wide.

### Japanese clethra

*Clethra barbinervis*

A handsome backdrop for white flowers, Japanese clethra is a shrub with deep green foliage and attractive, peeling bark. Throughout the summer, it produces fragrant white flowers in arching racemes. In the fall, its leaves turn bronze-red. Hardy to Zone 5. 10' tall × 10' wide.

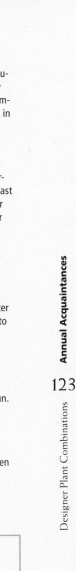

## *designer tips*

## Save Your Tuberous Tropical Annuals

Tropical tuberous plants like caladiums and dahlias can easily be overwintered and replanted the following year. Reduce water in autumn (cut the dahlia back to six inches), dig up tubers after the first frost, remove soil, and store them in a cool dry place (boxes of damp vermiculite or sand work well) between 55°F and 61°F.

# COASTAL ESCAPE

Like many garden unions, this planting is of mixed heritage. Garden designer Dave Buchanan, who specializes in gardens featuring California native plants, designed a garden brimming with jewels like California poppy and miniature lupine around his client's beach-town cottage. Augmenting the natives, his clients innocently planted a little western Mediterranean daisy, mini marguerite, which escaped into the native planting and formed a small sea of low-growing white daisies punctuated by the blue spires of lupine and California poppy. The resulting unplanned hybrid planting makes for an impressive spring display — proof that sometimes you cannot contain and control beauty. Every now and then, beauty just happens.

*Brimming with jewels like California poppy and miniature lupine*

### Mini marguerite daisy
*Chrysanthemum paludosum*
A vigorous little bedding plant for coastal and desert gardens, the white, daisylike flowers resemble a small Shasta daisy. The deeply toothed green foliage lends a lush feel to this great little plant. It's mostly grown as a summer annual, although it overwinters in mild climates. Likes full sun. It does spread, so be warned. 8"–10" tall × 8" wide.

### Miniature lupine
*Lupinus bicolor*
Awesome in coastal sage scrub areas, miniature lupine likes full sun and will thrive without watering in sunny, open areas. Like other lupines, miniature lupine fixes nitrogen in the soil so that surrounding plants will benefit. For the best way to start the hard-coated seeds, see A Trick for Growing Lupine from Seed, which works for many lupine species. Annual. 4"–6" tall × 6" wide.

### California poppy
*Eschscholzia californica*
California poppies are the quintessential Golden State wildflower, but their popularity in gardens extends clear to Great Britain. With orange, yellow, and occasionally cream-colored flowers borne above ferny foliage, Cal poppies love poor, sandy, well-drained soils but will tolerate richer garden soils as well. Their long, sickle-shaped seedpods explode when ripe. In cold climates, sow California poppy seeds in spring. In warm-weather climates, fall sowing is best. Annual. 12" tall × 6" wide.

## *designer tips*

## A Trick for Growing Lupine from Seed

Lupines, which are almost always grown from seed, have seeds that seem as hard as steel ball bearings. To get them to germinate, boil some water, pour it into a mason jar, and drop the seeds into it for an overnight soak to promote swelling. After the seeds have swollen, they are ready to sow in the garden.

# Phi Beta Butterfly Pink

If you've always wanted a rose-colored garden, this planting could put you, quite literally, in the pink. At Longwood Gardens in Pennsylvania, designers begin their pink garden with heat-loving annuals. Tropical 'Athens Rose' lantana and *Gomphrena* 'QIS Carmine' are planted in front of a perennial backdrop of burgundy purple fountain grass and mauve Joe-pye weed. With the lantana and joe-pye weed, this collection is bound to attract butterflies like fraternity brothers to a tapped keg.

### 'Athens Rose' hybrid lantana
*Lantana 'Athens Rose'*

A plant that thrives on neglect, 'Athens Rose' should be kept in full sun to produce multitudes of butterfly-attracting, magenta and creamy yellow flowers. When crushed, its rough-textured leaves are highly aromatic — a pleasant smell you will not soon forget. Hardy to Zone 8 (annual elsewhere). 2'–3' tall × 2'–4' wide.

### 'QIS Carmine' globe amaranth
*Gomphrena haageana 'QIS Carmine'*

Developed for the cut flower trade, this long-stemmed globe amaranth is the first with carmine pink flowers that are shaped like little drumsticks. A good heat-loving annual that, as a bonus for gardeners, has a long vase life. 45 days from seed. Annual. 24"–26" tall × 6"–10" wide.

### Purple fountain grass
*Pennisetum setaceum 'Rubrum'*

This dense, clumping grass with reddish purple blades and rose-colored plumes gives the combination a spot of darker red tones. The arching foxtail-like plumes are very attractive against the joe-pye weed. The selection 'Rubrum' does not usually set seed, although straight *P. setaceum* is considered an invasive weed in hot climates. Hardy to Zone 9. 3' tall × 18" wide.

### Joe-pye weed
*Eupatorium purpureum*

Joe-pye weed's vanilla-scented leaves (when crushed) are part of its appeal, but more than the leaves, its domelike, pink flowers borne on tall stems are what secure its place at the back of this design. Full sun to part shade. Hardy to Zone 5. 7' tall × 2'–4' wide.

### Mexican hyssop
*Agastache mexicana*

Although the pink agastache featured in this photo is an unidentified hybrid, Mexican hyssop, a recently introduced hardy hybrid, would fit nicely in this design, providing tubular pink and salmon-colored flowers. Regular soil and water requirements. Full sun or afternoon shade in the hottest climates. Hardy to Zone 5. 20" tall × 6" wide.

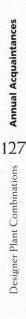

*designer tips*

## Intersperse Grasses for a Contemporary Look

Including ornamental grasses like purple fountain grass in perennial borders lends a fresh face to the traditional border by providing strong blades that would not be found in Victorian plantings. In many cases, this planting can give the vignette a more contemporary feel.

Designer Plant Combinations

128

A thick carpet of moss verbena (*Verbena pulchella*) combines with the ferny foliage and flashy orange flowers of California poppy (*Eschscholzia californica*) in this Dan Caudillo garden in Albuquerque.

# A Flash of Red on the Blue Mountainside

In a garden full of hardy perennials, the most important plant in spring just might be a flash-in-the pan annual — the Oriental poppy. Garden photographer, author, and plantswoman Karen Bussolini describes her garden as "a deer-infested mountainside full of plants that have survived the neglect of a photographer who is always away during peak garden season." At the center of this cool silver-blue and hot red assortment sits a glacial boulder the size of a Volkswagen bus. Planted around the monumental rock are 'Robusta' rose (espaliered to the boulder) underplanted with 'Six Hills Giant' catmint. In the foreground, purple-blue spikes of 'May Night' sage and intense blue flowers of 'Crater Lake Blue' veronica complete the cool side of the color palette. Adding a hot punch of color to the design, the vivid red Oriental poppy 'Türkenlouis' hovers over the 'May Night'. It should be noted that in her Kent, Connecticut, garden, Karen doesn't water any of these plants after they are established.

> *With silver plants as a backdrop, the garden can absorb all the color you throw at it.*

*designer tips*

## Use Silver Foliage Plants with Blues and Reds

Bussolini, who coauthored a book titled *Elegant Silvers*, suggests using "silver plants for both contrast and to harmonize." With silver plants as a backdrop, the garden can absorb all the color you throw at it. Also, many silver plants are deer resistant. As Bussolini says, "As the deer get worse and my time to take care of the garden decreases, my interest in silvers has only increased."

### 'Big Ears' lamb's ears
*Stachys byzantina* 'Big Ears'
In Karen's garden, 'Big Ears' lamb's ears is a workhorse. She uses it to suggest downhill flow on her steep hillside. The cultivar 'Big Ears' is synonymous with the cultivar 'Helene von Stein' and is more tolerant of high humidity and less prone to summer dieback. Hardy to Zone 4. 10" tall × 24" wide.

### 'May Night' sage
*Salvia* × *sylvestris* 'May Night' ('Mainacht')
The large, indigo flower spires of 'May Night' add a vertical element to complement the nearby poppy stems. Hardy to Zone 5. 28" tall × 18" wide.

### 'Six Hills Giant' catmint
*Nepeta* 'Six Hills Giant'
Karen loves tough plants and describes catmint as one of the "mainstays of my garden, repeated everywhere because it is so carefree." The nepeta, whose odor repels deer, protects the rose. Its gray-green color mediates between brighter silvers and greens; it's a fine foil for just about any color. Nepeta also blooms for about a month and reblooms after being cut back. Its foliage lasts well into December, and it attracts bees, beneficial insects, butterflies, and hummingbirds as well as hummingbird moths. Hardy to Zone 3. 36" tall × 24" wide.

### 'Crater Lake Blue' speedwell
*Veronica austriaca* subsp. *teucrium* 'Crater Lake Blue'
With true-blue flowers on numerous erect stems, 'Crater Lake Blue' veronica pairs nicely with 'May Night' sage and other purple-blue plants. Like most veronicas, it enjoys well-drained soil. Hardy to Zone 4. 36" tall × 24" wide.

### 'Türkenlouis' Oriental poppy
*Papaver orientale* 'Türkenlouis'
A large, fringed, orange-red fellow, 'Türkenlouis' is a full-size, sexy poppy that is the perfect hot temperature for all of the cool blues around it. Its neon intensity screams "look at me" while also calling attention to the similarly colored rose behind it. Hardy to Zone 3. 30" tall × 18"–24" wide.

### 'Robusta' rugosa rose
*Rosa rugosa* 'Robusta'
This tremendously hardy and vigorous Canadian rose echoes, in a slightly different hue, the red tones of the poppies in the foreground. This stiff-stemmed and thorny rugosa rose has deep green, leathery leaves and clusters of single, claret red flowers. This rose is the only non-deerproof plant in Bussolini's garden, but because of its proximity to catmint, the deer leave it alone when the catmint is growing. Hardy to Zone 5. 5' tall × 3' wide.

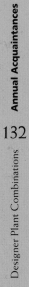

A cold-hardy 'Homestead' purple verbena (*Verbena canadensis* 'Homestead Purple') purple gathers around the rust-colored leaves of a coleus (*Solenostemon* sp.).

# MAKING ROOM FOR MERLOT LETTUCE

Most gardeners practice a strict brand of segregation between their vegetables and ornamental plants, but in horticulturist and writer Nancy Ondra's garden, she concocts a planting scheme of 'Merlot' lettuce and 'Margarita' sweet potato vine without a second thought. This whimsical little planting is unusual in that it incorporates lettuce into a mostly ornamental bed — a cottage-garden technique (interspersing vegetables with ornamentals) that is much talked about and seldom practiced. Because the lettuce is allowed to flower and set seed, it takes on a wholly different role here, becoming little, upright, burgundy towers topped with delicate, flowering candelabras. For those of you bent on segregating your ornamentals and vegetables, Nancy Ondra's planting encourages you to think again.

## designer tips

# Barberry Substitutes

Purple foliage makes a great backdrop for bright flowers and foliage, but keep in mind that barberries can reseed and are considered invasive in some parts of the country. For a similar effect with a less troublesome plant, Ondra suggests a purple-leaved smoke tree (*Cotinus coggygria*) such as 'Velvet Cloak' or summer wine ninebark (*Physocarpus opulifolius* 'Seward').

### 'Margarita' sweet potato vine
*Ipomoea batatas* 'Margarita'

One of the chartreuse-leafed selections of sweet potato vine, 'Margarita' is great for a quick, electric-green ground cover. You can almost watch sweet potato grow from its carbohydrate-packed tuber in warm weather. Hardy to Zone 11; grown as an annual most everywhere. 6" tall × 10'–20' wide.

### 'Merlot' lettuce
*Lactuca sativa* 'Merlot'

Like its viticulture namesake, 'Merlot' is deep and dark and full of antioxidants. It's one of the very darkest lettuces you can grow, and its shiny leaves and nonbitter taste make it a good bet for the veggie and show garden. 55 days to germinate from seed. Annual. 12" tall × 8" wide.

### 'Superba' barberry
*Berberis* × *ottawensis* 'Superba'

A brawny garden workhorse, 'Superba' barberry is a vigorous contender at the back of the bed. In this display, it forms a purple-red backdrop for the sweet potato vine, and its less-glossy leaves contrast nicely with the frillier and more lustrous lettuce leaves. Barberry is a much-used landscape plant, and its yellow spring flowers and desirable autumn crimson foliage are two of its assets. In some climates, barberry can be invasive (see Barberry Substitutes). Hardy to Zone 4. 8' tall × 8' wide.

*Like its viticulture namesake, 'Merlot' is deep and dark and full of antioxidants.*

# ACCENT PLANT
## Associates

One way to describe accent plants is to say they're plants that do not rely on flowering to generate interest in a garden. Accent plants seem muscular and confident, more physical and assertive than other plants. They are undoubtedly the sexiest of all the plant categories, and like grasses, their allure has captured the attention of designers across the country. Accents consist of succulent plants such as agaves, yuccas, and cactus as well as many other long-lived, sculptural garden plants. These plants are usually evergreen or eversilver, as the case may be, and maintain a year-round presence in the garden.

Some plants, such as the Midwest-native perennial rattlesnake master (*Eryngium yuccifolium*), are difficult to categorize. It *looks* like an accent, and in fact, its silver yucca-like leaves (hence its species name, *yuccifolium*) are a pretty fine imitation of pale-leaf yucca (*Y. pallida*). Even though the rattlesnake master passes muster in most respects as an accent, it is herbaceous — it goes dormant in the winter, therefore throwing it back into the perennial genre. Because I design gardens in Arizona,

accent plants like agaves, sotols (*Dasylirion*), yuccas, and prickly pears (*Opuntia*) are my stock-in-trade, but the interest in assimilating these bold plants into gardens stretches from Oregon to Boston. You can imagine my surprise to discover two of the groupings featured in this chapter — a beaked yucca (*Y. rostrata*) and stand of prickly pear cactus, some of my desert standards — thriving in a garden outside Philadelphia.

As the trend toward more contemporary architecture in this country gains steam, so will the use of accent plants. They are the living sculptures of our gardens, architectural in the best sense of the word. This is not to say that traditional homes and gardens should eschew a well-placed century plant; accent plants, which are often symmetrical, lend themselves equally well to traditional plantings and avant-garde situations. Perhaps best of all, accents seem to pull themselves up by their own bootstraps. They think nothing of you leaving them for a week's vacation without water — they will welcome you home just as happy as when you left.

At Ground Xero in Austin, Texas, Nancy Webber combines two drought-tolerant selections, white velvet (*Tradescantia sillamontana*) and Weber's agave (*Agave weberi*).

# New Agave and Yucca Frontiers

Long considered iconic plants of the Southwest, cold-hardy agaves are breaking new ground in gardens from Santa Fe to Philadelphia. In this shimmering combination, the lynchpin is a pair of ghostly gray Parry's agaves perched atop a rocky outcrop. From this vantage point, Parry's agave reigns over the snow-in-summer and is surrounded by an assortment of pink 'Ava' hummingbird mint, a variety whose deep rose flowers are the perfect backdrop for silver plants. Upslope from the Parry's agave, on another mound, is a cluster of banana yucca, which mirrors the star shapes of the agave and is one of the most durable and underused yuccas in horticulture.

*Iconic plants of the Southwest, cold-hardy agaves are breaking new ground in gardens.*

### Parry's agave
*Agave parryi*
One of the most cold hardy of all agaves, Parry's is a silver crown in the garden. Its silver-blue, heavily toothed rosettes demand attention. Parry's produces numerous offsets (baby plants that emerge from around its base), which can be transplanted easily. Like many members of the woody lily family, Parry's agave needs a long, warm season for establishment, so avoid fall planting in Zones 5 and 6; plant instead after the last frost in spring. Hardy to Zone 5. 24" tall × 30" wide.

### 'Ava' hummingbird mint
*Agastache* × 'Ava'
Breeding hummingbird mints has long been a specialty at High Country Gardens where David Salman plays with hybrids; so when he named one after his wife, Ava, the gardening world paid attention. 'Ava' (the hummingbird mint) is a hybrid between *A. cana* and *A. barberi*. In all respects, this is a superior hummingbird mint. Its main virtue is the unusual coloration of its calyxes, which maintain their deep rose color after blooming until frost, creating an extremely long season of color. 'Ava' likes amended, well-drained soil and looks best with one midspring shearing. Hardy to Zone 5. 4' tall × 24" wide.

### Snow-in-summer
*Cerastium tomentosum*
This very silver, and very tough — bordering on rampant — ground cover works well between rocks and as a carpet around drought-tolerant accent plants. From late spring through early summer — as its name suggests — it becomes covered with star-shaped white flowers. Hardy to Zone 3. 12–24" tall × indefinite width.

### Banana yucca
*Yucca baccata*
Not only is banana yucca hardy and structural, it has been an immensely useful plant stretching back to prehistoric times. Banana yucca fibers were used to make, among other items, sandals, baskets, rope, belts, bowstrings, and fishing nets. As if those uses were not enough, Native Americans also made a shampoo from the roots and cooked with the fleshy, sickle-shaped flowers. In the garden, two of the most appealing attributes of banana yucca are the white curling filaments that run along its leaf margins and its robust, durable nature. Provide full sun and good drainage. Hardy to Zone 4. 4' tall × 6' wide.

---

## designer tips

### Make a Rocky Yucca Outcrop
Many gardens have significant geology within their boundaries. Yucca species enjoy growing near rocks. To build a convincing rocky knoll in your garden, carefully place (do not pile!) good-size boulders by submerging each rock by at least one-third below grade. Odd numbers of rocks (one, three, or five) often look best. Leave nooks and crannies for plants that like quick drainage.

# ON THE DRY SIDE

On the edge of a low mound, horticulturist Laurel Voran fashioned an undulating carpet of exceptionally drought-tolerant and vibrant plants. Because these plants appreciate quick drainage, she began by amending the soil with lots of sand and gravel. For the color theme, Voran chose one of her favorites: yellow and fuchsia. And for a quirky structural touch, a prickly pear elbows its way into the arrangement, adding some vertical interest. The whole planting, which is at Chanticleer in Wayne, Pennsylvania, would be equally at home in El Paso, Texas.

## designer tips

### Don't Give Up on Your Prickly Pears!

Chanticleer horticulturist Laurel Voran loves her prickly pear, but she admits candidly that in the Mid-Atlantic states "opuntias look horrible during the winter and into early spring." She encourages gardeners to "be patient, don't worry, and don't pet them." The advice against petting comes from the experience of getting prickly pear glochids (fine hairlike stickers) on her hands. To remove glochids, use duct tape, a dot of white glue, or the edge of a credit card.

*Voran fashioned an undulating carpet of vibrant plants.*

**Hardy ice plant**
*Delosperma cooperi*
Ideal for planting in gravel mulch, hardy ice plant spreads itself out like a carpet of green beans. Throughout the summer, this South African native sports glossy, purple-magenta daisies, at times so dense that they obscure the foliage. Stop watering in fall (if you are watering it at all) to harden it off for winter. Hardy to Zone 5. 3" tall × 18" wide.

**'Comanche Campfire' evening primrose**
*Oenothera macrocarpa* 'Comanche Campfire'
This impressive, heat-loving evening primrose from western Oklahoma has not only sizable yellow flowers but also crimson red petioles and stem tips that give it its campfire designation. Its silver leaves also recommend it as a great rugged and drought-tolerant garden plant. Hardy to Zone 4. 15"–18" tall × 18"–24" wide.

**Sprawling prickly pear**
*Opuntia phaeacantha*
With pads shaped like Mickey Mouse ears and formidable, yellow spines, this accent plant distinguishes itself from its companions, providing a bold look and, as Voran says, "a bit of discouragement to anyone who may be tempted to tromp up the slope." It produces lovely waxy, yellow to orange flowers in early summer. Needs fast drainage and full sun (a south-facing slope is good). Avoid winter watering. Hardy to Zone 5. 18" tall × 2'–6' wide.

# CORDYLINE SERPENTINE

This two-plant wonder from designer Lynden Miller is a prime example of how weaving together two dissimilar plants can generate another dimension of interest in a planting. Occupying a prominent corner next to paving, deep blue Durand's clematis threads its tendrils through 'Red Sensation' false dracaena in an S-curve that recalls the movement of a snake through branches. Beyond the vastly contrasting textures of the two plants, the success of this combination has much to do with the reds Miller selects. Both the false dracaena and the clematis are deep purples that list toward the blue side of the spectrum, making them eminently compatible with each other.

*A diminutive, yet achingly beautiful vining plant*

**'Red Sensation' false dracaena**

*Cordyline australis* 'Red Sensation'

Growing from a central rosette that over time becomes a small trunk, the cool red leaves of 'Red Sensation' are architectural yet not as lethal as those of similarly shaped yuccas. As shown here, it makes a great spherical trellis on which to train delicate vines. Hardy to Zone 8 and the warmer parts of Zone 7. 48" tall × 18" wide.

**Durand's clematis**

*Clematis × durandii*

This petite climber is just the right size for climbing over small garden ornaments or, even better, over plants with bold foliage. An herbaceous clematis with deep purple-blue, four-petaled flowers, it's much sought after for training up small objects like tree stumps in the garden. Plant in deep, rich soil with regular moisture. Try it as featured here, intertwined with bold vertical plants like cordylines, agaves, and yuccas. Hardy to Zone 5. 3'–5' tall × 6" wide.

## designer tips

## Vines in Plants and Trees

It's a very Zen idea really: sneak a diminutive yet achingly beautiful vining plant within the superstructure of a larger architectural plant, like an elegant surprise. The same affect can also be accomplished by growing vines in trees. The trick is to choose vine species that are small and delicate so they won't strangle or otherwise overwhelm the tree. Herbaceous vines (those that die back in winter) like Durand's clematis are a good choice because their winter dormancy gives the tree a break from competition for part of the year.

# ROUND MOUNDS FOR PLANT HOUNDS

144

One of the best garden design tricks is using similarly shaped plants to generate a sense of repetition and rhythm in a space. In this grouping, the theme is the mound. Chanticleer horticulturist Laurel Voran uses lavender, beaked yucca, and 'Siskiyou Blue' fescue — all mound-shaped plants — and arranges them like overstuffed ottomans behind other drought-tolerant plants. As Voran exclaims, "Ahhh, repeated shapes!" Voran goes on to remark, "Using mounds of varying sizes and textures just works. I love simplicity in contrast to more detailed and fussy areas." It is interesting to note that while this combination is planted in metropolitan Philadelphia, it would be equally if not more successful in much of the western United States, particularly in arid regions.

## Plant a Yucca for Finery Relief

If you squint at your garden, does everything look like a blur of indistinct greenery? If so, the antidote may well be a large yucca such as the beaked yucca. A covey of fluffy or fussy perennials can often be rescued by a big, upright, bold plant placed front and center that will make all garden visitors say, "Now what have we got here?"

*Fussy perennials can often be rescued by a big, upright, bold plant.*

### 'Siskiyou Blue' fescue
*Festuca 'Siskiyou Blue'*

This tufty little nugget with blue spruce–colored leaves and a dense compact form populates the front border of this set. It will take full sun or part shade and is drought tolerant, and its unusually uniform ghostly blue leaves make it a front-of-the-border favorite. 'Siskiyou Blue' is a hybrid between the western native *Festuca idahoensis* and the nonnative *Festuca glauca*. With longer leaves than the more common *Festuca glauca*, 'Siskiyou Blue' has a softer, less sea-urchiny look than its parent. It produces beautiful, arching, tawny seed heads. Hardy to Zone 4. 2' tall × 2' wide.

### Creeping thyme
*Thymus praecox* subsp. *arcticus*

Enjoying the sunny site and fast drainage of its location, creeping thyme does as it is wont to do and spreads out a low and dense mat of fragrant foliage topped with pink-lavender flowers. It will take light foot traffic and can even be used as a lawn substitute or between cracks in rockwork, but in this instance, it is simply a low green-and-pink carpet that, despite its diminutive stature, is as tough and water-wise as all of its adjacent companions. Hardy to Zone 5. 2" tall × 24" wide.

### Hardy ice plant
*Delosperma cooperi*

Smack in the middle of this cluster, hardy ice plant provides some fuchsia relief from all of the surrounding silver-toned plants. Throughout the summer, this South African native sports glossy, purple-magenta daisies at times so dense that they obscure the foliage. Stop watering in fall (if you are watering it at all) to harden it off for winter. Hardy to Zone 5. 3" tall × 18" wide.

### Beaked yucca
*Yucca rostrata*

Among gardeners, beaked yucca has become one of the most sought after of the woody lilies. It is a handsome brute that won't be passed over by anyone with an appreciation for sculptural plants. Its narrow, blue leaves, stout trunk, and showy plume of cream-colored flowers in the summer count as considerable assets; perhaps that is why the plant pops up in some of the best gardens in the country from Boise to Austin to Philadelphia. As long as the drainage is good, beaked yucca will grow in full sun to part shade. Hardy to Zone 5. 10' tall × 4' wide.

### California fuchsia
*Zauschneria californica*

Although orange-red, trumpet-shaped flowers explode at the tips of California fuchsia in late summer, its low-mounding profile and hairy, silvery, lance-shaped leaves make it interesting throughout the warm season. As a hummingbird attractor, it most certainly lives up to its name. Hardy to Zone 6. 12" tall × 20" wide.

### 'Grosso' French lavender
*Lavandula* × *intermedia* 'Grosso'

The strongly scented flowers are perfect for craft or culinary use. 'Grosso' is also the most cold hardy of the French hybrids and is also more moisture tolerant than other lavenders, which is a plus for gardeners who have difficulty overwintering plants from this genus. Hardy to Zone 5. 30" tall × 24"–30" wide.

## PRICKLY PEARS AND FIREWHEELS

Coupling cactus and perennials takes a little planning. The main considerations are providing good drainage and selecting perennial species that will tolerate an infrequent watering regime in order not to drown the cactus. Here, I've used a substantial member of the prickly pear family in the middle of the planting, where it can stick its Mickey Mouse ears above flowering plants. To contrast with the blue-gray pads of the prickly pear, the bold red-and-yellow-tipped daisies of firewheel (*Gaillardia pulchella*) are well suited to the purpose.

## designer tips

## Working Around Prickly Plants

When gardeners get pricked by plants like agaves, it's usually because they aren't using the right protective equipment. Working with barbed plants can be fun and painless when you use the right tools. Prickly pear pads should be pruned using long-handled saws; weeding should be done with extra-long surgical tweezers; and young plants should be handled by their roots while wearing thorn-proof gloves.

### Engelmann's prickly pear
*Opuntia engelmannii*

Engelmann's prickly pear is a common and tenacious plant in most of the Southwest. In spring, showy yellow flowers appear. In late summer, its dark red fruit can be harvested and made into juice, jelly, or candy. Although Engelmann's prickly pear will spread out in a wide circle if left to its own devices, it can be kept much smaller by pruning off pads. Hardy to Zone 8. 6' tall × 10' wide. *Note:* For colder climates, try the smaller beavertail cactus (*Opuntia basilaris*), which blooms shocking pink flowers and is hardy to Zone 7. In wetter eastern climes, use *Opuntia humifusa*, which is hardy to Zone 5.

### Firewheel
*Gaillardia pulchella*

Firewheel is easily grown from seed sown in early spring; alternatively, you can purchase containerized specimens. The plant is bushy and enjoys lean to moderately rich soil. In the low-desert Southwest, firewheel will bloom from late spring through summer. In most other regions, it blooms from midsummer through fall. Plant breeders have lately introduced several new varieties of firewheel. Two notables include the intensely orange 'Oranges and Lemons' and a flower with fluted rays, 'Fanfare'. Hardy to Zone 5. 18"–24" tall × 15"-18" wide.

*Its dark red fruit can be harvested and made into juice, jelly, or candy.*

# THE NEON ENTRY

On the way to a front door, nothing says welcome quite like a dazzling clump of red-yellow kangaroo paw surrounded by purple-pink succulents, tiny geraniums, and yellow sedum. While this combination is not fully appreciated from the curb, it reveals itself as a neon surprise for visitors who approach the front door. Designer Scott Spencer uses rocks effectively to frame and highlight the planting, which contains a nice balance of upright, low-growing, and rosette-shaped plants. Because this combination is in southern California, I have listed more cold-hardy substitutes for gardens in less Mediterranean climates.

## designer tips

### Nestle Your Succulents in Rockery

One way to ensure that the roots of your succulent plants are well drained is to wedge them into landscape rocks, as Scott Spencer has done here. This technique works best if your landscape rocks are buried by one-third their height, rather than simply plopped on the ground.

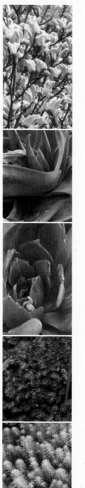

### Red-yellow kangaroo paw
*Anigozanthos* 'Harmony'

This stunning, tall evergreen perennial from Australia attracts the attention of humans and hummingbirds alike. From a base of swordlike leaves, four- to six-foot red bloom stalks with golden flowers emerge in late spring. Give red-yellow kangaroo paw full sun and well-drained soil. Hardy to Zone 10. 4'–6' tall × 2'–3' wide.
*Note:* In colder climates, overwinter the kangaroo paw indoors or substitute hesperaloe (*Hesperaloe parviflora* 'Yellow'; hardy to Zone 5).

### Coral aloe
*Aloe striata*

With pink-tinged leaf margins, the gray foliage of this South African native provides year-round interest to this planting. In late winter (in warm climates), coral aloe shoots up candelabra-like stalks of coral-red flowers. Hardy to Zone 9. 2'–3' tall × 1'–2' wide.

### 'Afterglow' echeveria
*Echeveria* 'Afterglow'

Pink and lavender-gray leaves characterize this rosette succulent, which appreciates afternoon shade in desert areas. Likes well-drained soil. Hardy to Zone 10. 12" tall × 12"–16" wide.
*Note:* In colder climates, substitute Parry's agave (*Agave parryi*; hardy to Zone 5) for coral aloe and Texas tuberose (*Manfreda maculosa*; hardy to Zone 7) for 'Afterglow' echeveria.

### 'Pink Fairy Cascades' geranium
*Pelargonium ionidiflorum* 'Pink Fairy Cascades'

This trailing species geranium has strong pink flowers with good drought and disease tolerance and a nice scent. It is sometimes used in teas as a folk remedy and is perfect for lining walkways. Full sun and well-drained soil. Hardy to Zone 10; annual elsewhere. 6"–12" tall × 12" wide.

### 'Angelina' stonecrop
*Sedum rupestre* 'Angelina'

Great for sunny sites with poor soil, 'Angelina' lights up the front of this border, where it mingles with 'Pink Fairy Cascades' and 'Afterglow'. Hardy to Zone 4. 4"–6" × 12"–24" wide.

# No Irrigation? No Problem

Designer David Cristiani believes in the generous use of bold forms and uses irrigation only as "life support" in times of severe drought. In this planting scheme, comprising mostly Chihuahuan Desert plants, he uses gentle basins and berms to intercept and capture rainfall. Using a central prickly pear in a starring role with rock penstemon and dazzling damianita daisy as a strong supporting cast, Cristiani makes a convincing case that dry gardens can be beautiful. An advocate of using more cactus in gardens, Cristiani comments, "Just like roses and driving they can be dangerous, but when used thoughtfully, they symbolize the Southwest and offer year-round green."

*Gentle basins and berms intercept and capture rainfall.*

### Engelmann's prickly pear
*Opuntia engelmannii*

Engelmann's prickly pear is a common and tenacious plant in most of the Southwest. In spring, showy yellow flowers appear and are followed by large, red-black fruit, as seen here, that will persist until fall. In late summer, its bright red fruit can be harvested and made into juice, jelly, or candy. Hardy to Zone 8. 6' tall × 10' wide.
*Note:* For colder climates, try the smaller beavertail cactus (*Opuntia basilaris*), which blooms shocking pink flowers and is hardy to Zone 7. In wetter eastern climes, use *Opuntia humifusa*, which is hardy to Zone 5.

### Damianita daisy
*Chrysactinia mexicana*

Rabbitproof, fragrant, and extremely showy in spring and summer, it's no wonder that damianita daisy has become a favorite of designers throughout the Southwest. Its tiny, bright green, needlelike leaves form a small mounding plant that turns into a dome of gold in spring. The tiny gold daisies are so profuse that they obscure the foliage completely — the effect is so arresting that some have likened damianita daisy to a "nuclear gumdrop." Over time, damianita can become woody and slightly leggy. For this reason, a biennial hard shearing is a good practice. Plant in full sun or reflected heat in well-drained soil. Hardy to Zone 6. 2' tall × 2' wide.

### Rock penstemon
*Penstemon baccharifolius*

An unusual penstemon with short, almost shrubby, evergreen foliage and rose-red flowers, this Texas native tolerates drought and alkaline soil with grace. Its spring and summer bloom draws hummingbirds from afar. It likes full sun to part shade and will tolerate reflected heat. Excellent drainage is a must. Hardy to Zone 6. 2' tall × 3' wide.

*designer tips*

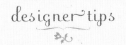

## Create a Dry Garden

In this vignette, David Cristiani has planted a dry garden in which the chosen plants will survive on rainfall alone after establishment. Rather than focusing on flowers, Cristiani prefers using what he calls "stronger" plants like long-lived cactus and shrubs to take over in heat, drought, and cold. His choice not only provides a bold look but also minimizes maintenance and future plant replacements at the edges of gardens.

# Enjoying Blue Shrimp with a Toothless Spoon

I've always been attracted to plant combinations that weave a delicate plant through the more upright, stiff structure of an accent plant, and this Brandon Tyson design illustrates how good the results of this knitting can look. He begins with a background of masculine, fan-shaped toothless spoon through which the delicate nodding heads of blue shrimp plant wander. The play of light coming through the toothless spoon and illuminating the blue shrimp plant is ethereal. The coup de grace in this planting is the large-flowered, fragrant angelica, whose glossy foliage fills in the space in the foreground and sends up its umbel-shape heads to add even more textural contrast to an already pleasantly contrasting composition.

## designer tips

### Pot-in-Pot Succulents

In regions where it's too cold to grow tender succulents like toothless spoon in the ground year-round, try growing them in nursery pots that you can place in the ground during the growing season and remove during winter. In well-drained soil, just dig a hole the width and the depth of your pot, place an empty pot (a five-gallon container, for example) in the hole as a sleeve, and then slide your succulent (still in its own five-gallon pot) into the sleeve. Hide the rims of the pots with gravel or organic mulch. If you have heavy soil, consider planting pot-in-pot in a mound for better drainage.

**Toothless spoon**
*Dasylirion quadrangulatum*
This symmetrical rosette of stiff, medium-green leaves is a Chihuahuan Desert relative of sotol (*Dasylirion wheeleri*). Extremely heat and drought tolerant, in warm regions it reaches massive proportions slowly, forming a sphere that resembles a sort of fiber-optic sculpture. As its name suggests, toothless spoon is free of the sawlike spines that line the margins of its cousin, sotol. Hardy to Zone 8. 10' tall × 6'–8' wide.

**Angelica**
*Angelica pachycarpa*
This is a true perennial angelica from the coasts of Spain and Portugal, one that plantswoman Annie Hayes (of Annie's Annuals in Richmond, California) calls "super tough and easy." Super shiny, almost varnished — or, as Brandon Tyson calls them, "licked" — leaves and russet-colored seed heads make it a hard plant to forget. In hot summer areas, it will go dormant and reappear with cooler fall temperatures. At maturity, its bloom spike may reach five feet tall. Self-sows freely. A great plant for winter greenery. Hardy to Zone 7. 3' tall × 3' wide.

**Blue shrimp plant**
*Cerinthe major 'Purpurascens'*
With blue-gray, clasping leaves on wiry stems and drooping purple-blue flowers, blue shrimp plant might be mistaken for oregano. This plant will seed around — and you should let it. It's as easy to move as a seedling. You have to hunt out the seeds, which remain inside the calyx, but giving the plant a good shake will release them. When blue shrimp plant starts to look ratty, just yank it out and new seedlings will fill in the gaps. Plant in full sun in well-drained soil. Hardy to Zone 5. 2' tall × 2' wide.

# FIGHTING SILVER WITH SILVER

If putting two tough, scrappy plants together is a good idea, you could do a lot worse than giant-flowered purple sage against a great star-shaped sotol, as designer David Salman has done here. The evergreen (or "eversilver," as the case may be) tones of the desert spoon provide the needed background for the giant-flowered purple sage. This is the perfect combo for hot, dry, rocky spots in the garden. Monochromatic silver planting schemes are sexier than stainless steel kitchen appliances, lending an edgy, hip aesthetic to your garden.

## designer tips

### Protect Young Sotol

Sotol, especially variet-
ies whose seed is collected
from populations in northern New Mexico, is a
cold-hardy brute; mature
specimens have thrived in
Zone 5. If you are push-
ing sotol's cold hardiness,
David Salman advises
planting young specimens
against a south-facing wall
after the last spring frost,
and then providing a thick
layer of protective mulch
for the first couple of
winters.

**Giant-flowered purple sage**
*Salvia pachyphylla*
Designer David Salman readily
admits that giant-flowered purple
sage is a highly variable plant.
"Some strains will have tall flower
spikes that tower over the foliage,
while others are compact." In this
combo, the taller variety is featured as the perfect companion
to desert spoon. Giant-flowered
purple sage likes full sun and
well-drained soils. Hardy to
Zone 5. 3' tall × 30" wide.

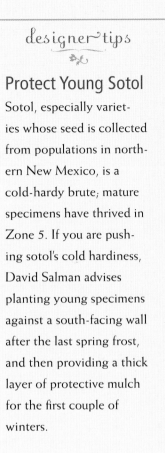

**Sotol**
*Dasylirion wheeleri*
The sotol is often mischaracter-
ized, made out to be more vicious
than it really is. True, its leaves
are armed like a double-edged
saw with small barbs, but the
pricks they give are shallow, and
the sheer sculptural power of the
plant's silver-blue rosette shape
is worth every drop of blood.
The plant requires virtually no
maintenance and will grow in
blasting sun without supplemental watering. All it needs is decent
drainage. Sotol's occasional 10-
foot-high, quill-like bloom spike is
an extra bonus. Hardy to Zone 6.
4' tall × 4' wide.

*Monochromatic silver planting schemes are sexier than stainless steel kitchen appliances.*

# A Pool of Silver Falls

It's hard to imagine how a plant could be better distinguished from its companions than this two-tone, deep green, center-stripe agave, which seems to pop out from a blanket of silver, an effect that designer Jonathan Wright takes some deserved pride in. "With a fountain nearby," Wright remarks, "it is almost like the agave is floating in a pool of water — like a water lily." The other plants in the cluster also suggest water — the true blue flowers of Sinaloa sage and the sky blue flowers of 'Heavenly Blue' southern star contribute to the conceit.

*It is almost like the agave is floating in a pool of water.*

### Center-stripe agave
*Agave lophantha*

Center-stripe agave forms large colonies and is so heat hardy that it is used in street median plantings in Arizona. The glossy leaves with a green-yellow center stripe are stiff and architectural, with armed margins and terminal tips. As featured here in Pennsylvania, it will stay smaller and probably not produce pups around the mother plant. It is native to Texas and Mexico and likes full sun to part shade and sharp drainage. Hardy to Zone 7. 2' tall × 3' wide.

### 'Heavenly Blue' southern star
*Oxypetalum caeruleum* 'Heavenly Blue'

This pale blue annual is a South American member of the milkweed family, which becomes obvious when you look at its bloated, banana-shaped seedpod. Great for hot situations, the little, sky-colored flowers hover over the plant and add to the illusion that the center-stripe agave is floating in water. This plant is a shrubby vine and can be overwintered as a houseplant. Annual. 24–36" tall × 24–36" wide.

### 'Silver Falls' dichondra
*Dichondra argentea* 'Silver Falls'

Forming the floor of this planting, the tiny silver leaves of 'Silver Falls' make an impressive, nearly metallic-looking cover and a fine backdrop for accent plants like the center-stripe agave. Tolerant of heat and poor soils. Hardy to Zone 9, but widely grown as an annual elsewhere. 3" tall × 3'–6' wide.

### Sinaloa sage
*Salvia sinaloensis*

This small blue sage with coppery-colored leaves works so well here because, like the center-stripe agave, it sticks up just enough from the sea of 'Silver Falls' to present itself as a miniature copper and blue bouquet. Hardy to Zone 7. 8"–12" tall × 8"–12" wide.

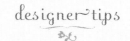

## designer tips

## How to Grow a Mat of 'Silver Falls'

'Silver Falls' has become a popular trailing plant for containers, but using it as a ground cover presents a challenge. Fortunately, though, it's one that's easily overcome. Because the stems are so long, wind can blow them into a tangled mess. To avoid this, heal in the middle of each stem — dig a little hole, bend the stem, and bury a short section, so the plant will root in and provide the solid cover you seek.

# GIANT SUCCULENT FLOWERS

With a cast of plump succulents, this pathside planting glows with blues and yellows. By creating a well-drained hillside, designer Scott Spencer is able to work his particular brand of southern California plant wizardry using plants with succulent blue and yellow coloration in both foliage and flower. The large blue rosettes of foxtail agave, pretty as giant flowers, serve as entry monuments, and the bright chartreuse gopher plant flowers are so vivid that they're almost like pathway lighting. Other vibrant yellows in this mix include Mexican tulip poppy and Mexican feather grass.

## designer tips

## Fast Drainage Equals Fast Growth

Unless he has a really great sandy loam to work with, Scott Spencer contours the gardens he designs for optimal drainage. "I use raised berms and mounds for my garden schemes," he says. "In my area, I frequently encounter heavy clay, and this method allows me to utilize plant material that I wouldn't be able to otherwise, especially in the heavy, poor draining soils I find after the developer compacts the site to make a building pad. The free-draining mounds allow my gardens to quickly establish and look grown in after only one season or less. Good soil and good drainage always yield good gardens."

*Good soil and good drainage always yield good gardens.*

### Foxtail agave
*Agave attenuata*
Growing from a large stem that sometimes arches over, foxtail agave can reach heights of four feet tall. Its thick trunk often produces offsets. In coastal California, the plant thrives in full sun, but inland and in low-desert areas, light shade helps foxtail agave keep its blue coloring. Hardy to Zone 11. 2'–4' tall × 3' wide.
*Note:* In colder climates, substitute pale-leaf yucca (*Yucca pallida*) for a similar blue rosette effect.

### Blue finger
*Senecio mandraliscae*
Spectacularly blue foliage and a spreading habit make this senecio well used in California gardens. Like foxtail agave, blue finger dislikes too much sun outside the coast. Hardy to Zone 10. 18" tall × 2' wide.
*Note:* In colder zones, try the stonecrop *Sedum cauticola* 'Lidakense' for an equally stunning, succulent ground cover with blue foliage. Hardy to Zone 4.

### Mexican feather grass
*Nassella tenuissima*
Its fine texture belies its true tough-as-nails nature. Although Mexican feather grass is a native of the southwestern United States, it has become a widely used landscape plant in gardens from California to Massachusetts, where it is used as an annual. In Santa Fe, Mexican feather grass is ubiquitous and seems to have become the town's self-appointed street-median grass. This speaks to its prodigious reseeding habit, which should not be underestimated. The good news is that Mexican feather grass seedlings are shallow rooted and easily pulled out. Hardy to Zone 5. 2' tall × 2' wide.

### Gopher plant
*Euphorbia rigida*
The long curving stems and broad clusters of chartreuse flowers in winter or early spring make this Mediterranean native highly sought after in gardens from Denver to Delaware. Because the stems die back after flowering, the spent stems are best removed in late spring. Plant in full sun or part shade. Gopher plant will reseed moderately. Hardy to Zone 5. 2'–3' tall × 2'–3' wide.

### 'Brilliant Blue' babiana
*Babiana stricta* 'Brilliant Blue'
Growing in a purple-blue clump just below the foxtail agave, 'Brilliant Blue' babianas contribute to the cool-colored planting. These fragrant South African bulbs are fall planted for early spring color. Hardy to Zone 8. 6"–10" tall × 8" wide.

### Mexican tulip poppy
*Hunnemannia fumariifolia*
Ferny blue-gray leaves and neon yellow blooms make this poppy family a natural for this blue-yellow assortment. Hardy to Zone 10; grown as annuals in colder climates. 24"–36" tall × 10" wide.

# GLOWING GRAY-GREENS

This rugged and naturalistic bunch is a lesson in getting over the color green. Instead of a deep green nod to the Northwest, designer Judith Phillips presents us with a study of olive, silver, and wheat colors that glow in the afternoon light and are perfect for dry gardens in the Intermountain West and beyond. The mounds of Apache plume, complete with their luminous feathery fruit, form the foundation of the planting, while the Mexican blue sage adds low, silver foliage and a stippling of blue flowers. Adding its spiny, mouse-eared shape, Engelmann's prickly pear, with its red-black fruit, contrasts boldly with the finer textures of the Apache plume and Mexican blue sage.

## designer tips

### Pruning for Youth and Vigor

Although this planting needs very little care, a little pruning (a couple of times a year) will go a long way toward keeping things in prime shape. Judith Phillips suggests trimming the spent flower stems of Mexican blue sage below the point where the leaves cluster on the stems. She also recommends removing the oldest stems of both the sage and the Apache plume down to the ground each spring to keep the plants young and vigorous and ensure that they bloom intensely.

### Apache plume
*Fallugia paradoxa*

One of a select few thornless, drought-tolerant shrubs, this Southwest native is all about the stems and fruit. Yes, it has leaves — small lobed things that sparsely line the stem — but the real show is the graceful, wheat-colored branches topped with hairy fruits that glow white and pink in the afternoon light. Because it grows up to elevations of 8,000 feet, it is very cold hardy. In all but the driest climates, it can be grown without irrigation after establishment. In the very hot low deserts, a deep monthly irrigation will suffice. Hardy to Zone 4. 4'–8' tall × 4'–8' wide.

### Mexican blue sage
*Salvia chamaedryoides*

Shimmering silver leaves, a low growth habit, and small, sapphirelike, true blue flowers characterize Mexican blue sage. While the heaviest blooming occurs in spring and autumn, Mexican blue sage will continue to produce flowers intermittently throughout the summer. Provide full sun for best results. Mexican blue sage seems to prefer clay soil as long as it isn't kept too wet. Hardy to Zone 8. 2' tall × 2' wide.

### Engelmann's prickly pear
*Opuntia engelmannii*

Engelmann's prickly pear is a common and tenacious plant in most of the Southwest. In spring, showy yellow flowers appear, followed by large, red-black fruit, as seen here, which persist into fall. In late summer, its bright red fruit can be harvested and made into juice, jelly, or candy. Hardy to Zone 8. 6' tall × 10' wide.
*Note:* For colder climates, try the smaller beavertail cactus (*Opuntia basilaris*), which blooms shocking pink flowers and is hardy to Zone 7. In wetter eastern climes, use *Opuntia humifusa*, which is hardy to Zone 5.

# TROPICAL ADVENTURES IN BURGUNDY

When Dan Benarcik, a crack horticulturist at Chanticleer in Wayne, Pennsylvania, put together this riotous and ornate assemblage of plants, he began by "choosing a color — deep burgundy — and using it in a flower, a foliage plant, and a plant with form." The results, while far from monochromatic, show the power of color in unifying diverse plantings. All of these plants have more or less tropical origins, appreciate full sun, and eschew hard freezes.

> *'Red Sensation' serves as an emphatic exclamation point, because of its long, swordlike leaves, arresting purple-red foliage, and symmetrical rosette shape.*

## 'Red Sensation' false dracaena
*Cordyline australis* 'Red Sensation'

'Red Sensation' takes a commanding position toward the front of the bed, where its strong form can be appreciated close up. Used as specimen, 'Red Sensation' serves as an emphatic exclamation point because of its long, swordlike leaves, arresting purple-red foliage, and symmetrical rosette shape. For those who enjoy growing hardy tropicals, false dracaena takes more cold than one might suspect, although it will stay much smaller in colder climates than it does in frost-free zones. Hardy to Zone 8 (and the warmer parts of Zone 7 with protection). 48" tall × 48" wide.

## Blood leaf
*Alternanthera dentata* 'Rubiginosa'

Under the swords of the false dracaena the blood leaf resides, putting a mass of burgundy at ground level. A tropical from the West Indies, blood leaf is a relative of the dye plant amaranth, and its leaves exhibit some of the same crimson pigmentation. The top surface of the leaf is a lustrous blue-purple, while the bottom is pure burgundy. Hardy to Zone 9; grown as an annual in colder zones. 8"–20" tall × 20" wide.

## 'Paul' sage
*Salvia splendens* 'Paul'

This hot-blooded Brazilian sage with wine-purple calyces is a hefty, exuberant garden plant that plays well with the foliage of the blood leaf and 'Red Sensation'. Hardy to Zone 9; grown as an annual in colder zones. 3' tall × 3' wide.

## Sweet hibiscus
*Abelmoschus manihot*

This great mallow-family plant with flowers completes the tropical theme. The sweet hibiscus's deeply lobed leaves are used for food and paper manufacture in Samoa and Japan, respectively. As shown here, the usefulness of the plant is relegated more to the boldness of its foliage and large, tropical flowers with burgundy eyes. Hardy to Zone 9; grown as an annual in colder zones. 4'–6' tall × 36" wide.

## designer tips

### Use the Three Fs: Flower, Foliage, and Form

As Dan Benarcik recommends, choose one good color and echo it in at least three different types of plants: a flowering plant, a foliage plant, and one with dramatic form. This recipe helps establish unity and variety, and is almost guaranteed to please.

# ¡Tequila!

Tequila, the Mexican national drink, is a big hit in North America. If designer Carrie Nimmer has anything to say about it, blue agave, the plant from which tequila is derived will achieve similar fame as a landscape plant north of the border. Nimmer, who is known to some of her friends as "Queen Agave," is a woman so entranced with agaves that she has suggested using them as substitutes for wedding bouquets. Here, where it plays the stalagmite to the stalactite of a blue palo verde branch, its position shows off the stiff and straight nature of the plant. The blue palo verde, with its glaucous leaves and pendulous branches loaded with highlighter-yellow blooms, is the perfect overlord for the blue agave.

The blue agave plays stalagmite to the stalactite of the blue palo verde branch.

**Blue agave**
*Agave tequilana*
You might guess that it would take a giant, brazen, saw-toothed blue plant to make such an intoxicating concoction, but you might not have expected it to be such an out-of-the-ordinary landscape plant. Its stiff, upright leaves, whose terminal spines and margins are outlined in black, make it one of the most architectural plants anywhere. Give it a warm spot, good drainage, and plenty of room. Hardy to Zone 9. 5' tall × 5' wide.

**Blue palo verde**
*Parkinsonia florida*
In habitat, its blue-green, arching branches sweep the ground. In spring masses of bright yellow flowers cover the tree and fall to the ground like a thick cloak. This spectacular and majestic tree has a green trunk and branches that are capable of photosynthesis in drought conditions. Plant in well-drained soil in full sun. Hardy to Zone 8. 30' tall × 30' wide.

## designer tips

### Layer with Weeping Specimens

Instead of always thinking of how plants will look side by side, consider how a specimen tree with a weeping habit (like blue palo verde) will look when draped over the plants below it. Another weeping combination for warm climates is the sweet acacia (*Acacia farnesiana*; hardy to Zone 7) draped over upright, sword-like leaves of giant hesperaloe (*Hesperaloe funifera*; hardy to Zone 6).

# Opposites Attract: Going for Maximum Contrast

When it comes to form, two plants could hardly be more different from Adam's needle yucca and 'Compact Red' coleus. High contrast is exactly what New York designer Lynden Miller was shooting for when she designed this planting. The deep velvety leaves of the coleus juxtaposed against the yucca's spikiness make for a subtle and unexpected pair — like a tender, young Boston socialite going out with a leathery Wyoming cowboy.

## designer tips

### Plant Like a Painter

Lynden Miller looks at plants with a painter's eye, which is part of the reason she uses reds in her groupings. "I love dark reds and use them wherever I can," she remarks. "As a painter originally, I know that the reds make the greens look greener, and the idea is to put things together that will enhance each other and give the heart a lift."

### Adam's needle
*Yucca filamentosa*

The most durable, widely available, and easy to grow of all the yuccas, Adam's needle always makes a bold statement in the garden. This member of the agave family is a clump-forming plant that will send up annual bloom stalks of nodding, cream-colored flowers that bolt from three to eight feet above the radiating, rosette foliage. Adam's needle is a yucca that usually forms offsets (or pups), especially when you cultivate around the plant's roots. As pictured here, in a small colony, Adam's needle is useful when left in clumps. Should the clumps grow too large, they can be easily divided. Hardy to Zone 4. 30" tall × 5' wide.

### 'Compact Red' coleus
*Solenostemon 'Compact Red'*

Popular for its velvety, deeply toothed leaves and vivid colors, coleus often provides a refined textural counterpoint to bold-textured plants. A highly bred plant, coleus is available in a mind-boggling array of cultivars with distinctive leaf color and shape. Here, 'Compact Red' serves as a deep burgundy cushion to the upright yucca. Coleus is easily propagated; cuttings root even in water. Provide rich, loose, well-drained soil. Grow as an annual, except in frost-free regions. 8"–12" tall × 8"–12" wide.

*The deep velvety leaves of the coleus juxtaposed against the yucca's spikiness make for an unexpected pair.*

# CREEPING THE FLAME ALIVE

Horticulturist Jonathan Wright loves using agaves, especially the larger forms, but he also recognizes that a toothy century plant with sharp terminal spines could come across as fearsome and intimidating when planted on its own. To soften the effect, he plants small annual vines like the Mexican flame vine pictured here and allows them to "ramble through the wide-spreading leaves." When the Mid-Atlantic heat gets cranking, the Mexican flame responds by producing lots of strong orange composite flowers that light up the space between agave leaves. The orange flowers and silver-blue foliage are a winning fire-and-ice juxtaposition.

## designer tips

### Soften Accent Plants with Sweet Peas

Earlier in the growing season, Jonathan Wright substitutes sweet peas for Mexican flame flower to soften the agave and give a flash of color and scent to the garden. When the sweet peas finish, the Mexican flame fills in through the summer.

**Century plant**
*Agave americana*
Agave expert Mary Irish describes this as "the most cosmopolitan of agaves, with the longest ornamental history." It is also one of the largest specimens, forming a giant plant with numerous pups at its base. At Chanticleer, in Wayne, Pennsylvania, Jonathan Wright overwinters century plant in a greenhouse until spring. Hardy to Zone 8. 4'–10' tall × 4'–13' wide.

**Mexican flame vine**
*Senecio confusus*
This vigorous heat lover is a great performer in hot weather, sending out drifts of hot orange flowers on its tendrils. Its fleshy, semisucculent leaves and tendrils twine out along the ground and will climb up structures (or other plants, as shown here) if allowed. Mexican flame vine's orange flowers look great against plants with blue-gray foliage like that of the century plant. Hardy to Zone 9; grown as an annual elsewhere. 6" tall × 10' wide (if untrellised).

*Strong orange flowers light up the space between agave leaves.*

Accent Plant Associates

169

Designer Plant Combinations

# WHEN MACHO MOCHA CAME TO TOWN

Sometimes you want a plant just because it has such a cool name. This could be the case with 'Macho Mocha' mangave — that is, until you actually *see* the plant, at which time you *must* have it. Designer Scott Spencer admits that he does not use many *Agave* genus plants in gardens — many are just too pokey for his clients — but he makes an exception for 'Macho Mocha' (whose agave parentage is in question; see the plant description). With the chocolate-dipped leaf tips of 'Macho Mocha' draping languidly over a rock wall, Spencer softens the look with the cheerful flowers of 'Sunspots' sundrops and 'Vera Higgins' stonecrop.

## designer tips

### Succulent Companions

By design, outsize succulents like 'Macho Mocha' are usually placed a fair distance apart. To fill the space between plants, you have two options: mulch the space with attractive gravel (succulents generally dislike organic mulches) or use compatible trailing plants to fill the gaps. If you choose plants, you can try other succulents — like blue finger (*Senecio mandraliscae*) or 'Vera Higgins' stonecrop — or tough, low-growing perennials that will survive on the same watering regime as the succulents, like prostrate rosemary (*Rosmarinus officinalis* 'Huntington Carpet').

### 'Macho Mocha' mangave
×*Mangave* 'Macho Mocha'

The interesting name, no doubt a result of the burly nature of the plant combined with the coffee-purple spots on its leaves, is also a very attractive plant. Introduced by Yucca Do nursery, the plant is thought to be a hybrid between *Manfreda variegata* and *Agave celsii* — hence the new genus name *Mangave*, although it is also sold as *Manfreda* × 'Macho Mocha' as well as *Manfreda variegata* 'Macho Mocha'. Despite the confusion about its name and parents, it has proved to be a delightful and unique spotted garden plant that is tolerant of a wide range of growing conditions from Austin to San Diego. Like its presumed parent, *Agave celsii*, it has rather soft leaf tips that will not skewer passersby. Hardy to Zone 8. 1.5' tall × 3' wide.

### 'Sunspots' sundrops
*Calylophus* 'Sunspots'

What can you say about a robust trailing plant with yellow primrose flowers and jet black eyes (the colors of a bumble bee) other than "Wow! I want some!" A native to central Texas, 'Sunspots' does just fine in rocky, poor soils and hot conditions. For best appearance, give it a good haircut early in spring. Often visited by hawk moths at twilight. Hardy to Zone 6. 16"–24" tall × 24"–36" wide.

### 'Vera Higgins' stonecrop
*Graptosedum* 'Vera Higgins'

Peeking out from under the 'Sunspots', the little bronze-red rosettes of 'Vera Higgins' add a small layer to the planting. In spring 'Vera Higgins' blooms four-petaled, yellow blooms, but the fleshy leaves are the most interesting aspect of the plant. Full sun in coastal climates to part shade in the desert. Hardy to Zone 10. Less than 1' tall × 1'–2' wide.

*The chocolate-dipped leaves of 'Macho Mocha' drape languidly over a rock wall.*

# STRONG PLANT MEDICINE

Lavender-blue whorls and pale yellow spires combine in this succulent and woody perennial pair, and when you begin with gray, yellow, and blue, it's hard to go wrong. Medicinal aloe provides a strong central focus while the more blousy, gray foliage of the Cleveland sage rises up behind and around it. This Carrie Nimmer–designed plant combo is not only aesthetically pleasing, but also is practical: the gel-like sap inside the fleshy leaves of medicinal aloe can be applied to burns and cuts, and the highly aromatic leaves and branchlets of Cleveland sage are often bundled together as a smudge stick and used as incense.

## designer tips

### Placing Fragrant Plants

Occasionally, letting your plants overhang a walkway can be a good thing. Plants like Cleveland sage release a noticeable scent when we brush against them. Because humans have a high percentage of brain cells devoted to smell, planting aromatic plants near walkways is one way to guarantee powerful memories of your garden.

*The aromatic leaves of Cleveland sage are often used as incense.*

**Medicinal aloe**
*Aloe barbadensis*
Also known as aloe vera, the fleshy and symmetrical blue-gray leaves of medicinal aloe make it a good accent for naturalistic plantings. Besides the medicinal value of the sap, the plant's tall, spearlike flower spikes add vivid color to the twosome, and the hundreds of trumpet-shaped, yellow blooms on each spike draw in the hummingbirds. Aloes need good drainage and will survive in full sun to part shade, although they tend to look best when protected from afternoon sun. Hardy to Zone 9. 2' tall × 3' wide.
*Note:* In colder climates, substitute 'Cleopatra' foxtail lily (*Eremurus* 'Cleopatra') for the aloe for a similar effect.

**Cleveland sage**
*Salvia clevelandii*
This California chaparral zone native is a fragrant and stout workhorse. Its silver leaves emit a strong and pleasant sage scent when we brush against them, and in late spring and early summer, Cleveland sage explodes with whorls (circular flowers stacked like shish-kabobs along its stems) of blue-violet flowers. Its robust size and silver leaves make it an excellent backdrop for yellow- or red-flowered plants. Provide excellent drainage. Hardy to Zone 7. 4'–6' tall × 4'–6' wide.
*Note:* In colder climates, try *Salvia pachyphylla*, which provides even more dense foliage than *Salvia clevelandii*, as well as glowing blue flowers whose calyces turn an iridescent purple.

# GREAT GOLDEN ORNATE

Sometimes it's best to forget pared-down simplicity and genteel colors and just go for it. Going for it is pre-cisely what designer Lynden Miller has done in this New York Botanical Gardens planting that wows with maximum plant density and seemingly gilded shades of gold and chartreuse interspersed with maroon. Spiky plants like 'White Beauty' eremurus quickly disabuse you of the notion that this is some sort of Victorian vignette. On the contrary, the bright colors and bold forms are a tour de force of color and form.

## designer tips

# Take a Small Area and Go Big!

With all the hype about low-maintenance gardening, some people seem to have forgotten the pleasures of planting, observing, and tending an intensely cultivated garden area like the display featured here. In your home garden, consider setting aside at least one area to plant an arrangement of show-stoppers, even if they require you to tend to them more than you are used to.

*This garden wows with maximum plant density.*

### 'Snowflake' oakleaf hydrangea
*Hydrangea quercifolia 'Snowflake'*
This exceptional cultivar bears double, white flowers. Here its long flower panicles echo, in a shorter package, the shape and color of 'White Beauty' foxtail lily. The leaves of 'Snowflake' turn maroon and purple in autumn, and its chocolate-brown bark is attractive in winter after it has lost its leaves. Plant in full sun to part shade in deep, moist soil. 'Snowflake' flowers for six to eight weeks in June and July. Hardy to Zone 5. 5'–8' tall × 5'–8' wide.

### Balloon flower
*Platycodon grandiflorus*
Although not yet in bloom in this photo, balloon flower's bright green globe shape makes for good form in the middle of the grouping. It's well-known, purple-blue flowers bloom in mid- to late summer. Plant in moist, well-drained soil. Suitable for rock gardens. Hardy to Zone 4. 24" tall × 12" wide.

### Golden catalpa
*Catalpa bignonioides 'Aurea'*
For large, bright gold, heart-shaped leaves, golden catalpa is hard to beat. The trick to keeping the leaves close to ground level and keeping the plant compact is a severe pruning each year. Hardy to Zone 4. 30' tall × 40' wide (much smaller with pruning).

### 'White Beauty' foxtail lily
*Eremurus 'White Beauty'*
These showy bulbs are among the most upright and architectural plants you can grow. They truly are like exclamation points in the garden. Grow in full sun with well-drained soil and protect from high winds. Hardy to Zone 5. 4'–5' tall × 12" wide.

### Tassel flower
*Emilia javanica*
The scarlet-orange flowers of annual tassel flower are borne on slender, wiry stems and are a nice complement to the 'Australia' canna beside it. Sow seeds indoors six weeks prior to last frost date. Annual. 18" tall × 6" wide.

### 'Australia' canna lily
*Canna 'Australia'*
Forming the burgundy centerpiece of this planting, this New Zealand native, with leaves so shiny and burgundy-black that they appear shellacked, is a very unusual canna. There are many cannas with red or striped foliage, but none quite so dark and lusty as 'Australia'. Hardy to Zone 7. 60" tall × 24" wide.

# GROUND COVER Groupies

Ground covers have a curious and inverse relationship with turf grass; the less grass in a garden, the more important ground covers become. And gardens with a diversity of ground covers are always more intriguing than a monoculture of lawn. Usually defined as spreading plants with a height of no more than 18 inches (and usually planted to cover large areas), ground covers can be used singly or en masse or artfully combined with others. Pairing up different ground covers can result in patterns as intricate as those found on Persian carpets.

Ground covers provide some of the same functions as turf — cooling bare soil, suppressing dust, and retaining soil — while providing a higher level of interest and lower maintenance than lawns. As a general rule, I advise clients that if the only time they spend on their turf involves mowing it, they might be better served by another sort of planting scheme; and usually that scheme includes ground covers. While most nonturf ground covers cannot withstand sports usage, many can be walked on without damage. Many of the ground covers featured in this chapter — especially the succulent ones — use less water than turf grass, an important consideration in arid parts of the country. In addition to this chapter, make sure to read Masses of Grasses (page 64), which should give you some other ideas about how to make bare earth disappear with plants.

Indian blanket (*Gaillardia pulchella*) and blue chalk fingers (*Senecio vitalis*) offer a colorful, drought-tolerant ground cover for warm climates.

Designer Plant Combinations

# THE POWER OF THREE

Landscape architects are sometimes criticized for massing together lots of the same plants together, but when a designer like Piet Oudolf gets his hands on three good plants, massing can work big time! In this planting, like many of his at Battery Park in New York City, he's working beneath sycamore trees in filtered shade and is therefore using a palette that will accommodate part sun. This grouping is pure genius — a curry-colored carpet of 'Caramel' coralbells punctuated by three military 'Lance Corporal' fleeceflowers with a virtual wall of 'Moorflame' purple moor grass backing it all up. What more could you ask for?

## designer tips

# Designing with Seed Heads in Mind

It used to be that good gardeners would be out with the pruning shears before two petals fell off a coneflower, but the movement toward more natural and organic forms in gardens has changed all that. As a pioneer of the New Wave garden movement, which advocates for an appreciation of plants not just for their flowers but also for the shapes they take throughout their lifecycles, Oudolf is a proponent of letting interesting seed heads stand in a garden — sometimes long after the blooms have passed.

This is not only an aesthetic practice for the garden, it's good for wildlife, particularly birds. Some of the plants he employs frequently for their seed heads (among other qualities) are compass plant (*Silphium laciniatum*), prairie dock (*Silphium terebinthinaceum*), pale purple coneflower (*Echinacea pallida*), and Jerusalem sage (*Phlomis fruticosa*).

*A curry-colored carpet of 'Caramel' coralbells punctuated by three military 'Lance Corporal' fleeceflowers*

**'Caramel' coralbells**
*Heuchera* 'Caramel'
The whole point of this plant is the foliage. This vigorous perennial is employed here as a ground cover, producing leaves the color of a dish of Indian masala. The tiny, pink flowers are nothing to write home about, and many gardeners who are using the plant as ground cover choose simply to cut them off as they emerge. Because one of the parents of 'Caramel' is southeastern United States native *Heuchera villosa*, 'Caramel' is tolerant of hot, humid summers if given ample water and a little shade. Hardy to Zone 4. 12"–18" tall × 24" wide.

**'Lance Corporal' fleeceflower**
*Persicaria virginiana* 'Lance Corporal'
With distinctive, burgundy, chevron leaf markings reminiscent of the insignia of a lance corporal, this fleeceflower rises up out of a sea of 'Caramel' coralbells with oomph. It sends up fuzzy, red flowers in August and September, but its leaves, which look a little like crimson clover, are a large part of the show. Hardy to Zone 5. 28" tall × 24" wide.

**'Moorflamme' purple moor grass**
*Molinia caerulea* 'Moorflamme'
Slender, arching, and exquisite, 'Moorflame' is a German selection of moor grass that turns an intense orange-red color in autumn. One of the best moor grass selections for its graceful upright form, here it stands like a fortress, making a fine foil for the plants in the foreground. Like most moor grasses, it prefers moist, well-drained soil and will tolerate sun to partial shade. Hardy to Zone 4. 4' tall × 2' wide.

# CURBSIDE COOL

In a narrow curbside bed between a sidewalk and asphalt driveway, Delaware Center for Horticulture plant artist Lenny Wilson has combined one semisucculent perennial with two heat-loving annuals in a concoction that will work in hot spots from Wilmington to Dallas. What is most attractive about this hell-strip planting is that these heat lovers have cool-spectrum foliage — and the silver-blue euphorbia and purple heart exude coolness without excessive thirst. As Wilson comments, "Passersby seem to adore the gray/maroon combo. These plants were selected for low maintenance and vivid color combinations. This is a full sun area with good drainage, and it bakes in the sun during the summertime."

## designer tips

### Enhance an Annual Flower Bed with Bulbs

To extend the season in a bed planted primarily with annuals, Wilson recommends the addition of bulbs. In the featured plant combination, the entire bed is underplanted with grape hyacinths, which contrast nicely with the chartreuse flowers of the euphorbia. After flowering, the euphorbia stems are cut back in late April to allow new foliage to emerge, and the bed is planted with the summer annuals that thrive in the heat and do not require much water.

### Myrtle spurge
*Euphorbia myrsinites*
The waxy, blue leaves, which radiate in spirals out from central stems, are one of the main draws of this tough little semisucculent perennial. Myrtle spurge is very similar to its close cousin, gopher plant (*Euphorbia rigida*), except that myrtle spurge is more compact, almost like a ground cover. The other attraction is the lime-green flowers that arrive at the tips of the plant in early spring. With purple heart by its side, there is no more potent color combination than blue-gray and deep purple. It should be noted that at higher elevations in the Intermountain West (particularly in Colorado), myrtle spurge is considered invasive. Hardy to Zone 5. 4" tall × 12" wide.

### Purple heart
*Tradescantia pallida* 'Purpurea'
A formidable trailing plant in warm climates, purple heart's leaves and stems turn a dark, rich purple, especially in full sun, and in summer, pairs of tiny, pink flowers appear at the stem ends. This plant is adaptable to cramped root conditions and drought. As Lenny Wilson says, "It flourishes in the hot months." In the hottest parts of the Southwest, it appreciates afternoon shade. In northerly climates, like at the Delaware Center for Horticulture, it is grown as a summer annual. Hardy to Zone 10. 8" tall × 16" wide.

### Rose moss
*Portulaca grandiflora* 'Yubi Red' and 'Yubi Yellow'
'Yubi' rose moss is a semisucculent annual that loves heat and will trail and flower in harsh conditions. Here, Lenny Wilson uses both red and yellow rose moss to sparkle up the cool-colored myrtle spurge and purple heart. Like the purple heart, rose moss is happiest in the hottest months. Annual. 6"–8" tall × 18" wide.

# The Zen of Wormwood and Ice Plant

You can call it "less is more" or "minimalism" or "Zen," but what a planting like this conveys is simplicity. Although the individual components are all clearly distinguishable — rock, hemispherical sage, blanket of ice plant — they meld together in an iconic planting that has a certain Japanese stillness, almost timelessness. The good news is that this durable template designed by Greg Foreman could be replicated with relative ease in many a pathside garden bed.

*Rock, sage, blanket of ice plant — form a planting with a Japanese stillness, almost timelessness.*

### 'Silver Mound' artemisia
*Artemisia schmidtiana 'Silver Mound'*
This compact hemispherical plant is aromatic, drought tolerant, and deer resistant. Like other artemisias, the main attraction is not the flowers, which are insignificant, but rather the silvery foliage, which in this case forms a near-perfect symmetrical dome. To keep the plant to a single mound, remove offsets and replant them elsewhere. Hardy to Zone 3. 12" tall × 12"–24" wide.

### Hardy yellow ice plant
*Delosperma nubigenum*
This ice plant forms a thick mat of succulent foliage with plump, bright green leaves that resemble baby toes. In the early spring, it will light up with bright yellow flowers. This South African native is drought tolerant, but it will need a bit more supplemental water than Turkish speedwell. Panayoti Kelaidis recommends providing it with afternoon shade in hot climates such as Albuquerque. Hardy to Zone 5. 2" tall × 3' wide.

---

## designer tips

### Recipe for a Zen Pathway Planting
For a pared-down Zen look along a pathway, limit yourself to three elements: choose a medium-size rock, an evergreen flowering ground cover, and a slightly taller symmetrical plant. Repeat this grouping in odd numbers and avoid lining up plants. Bury your rocks by one-third their total height.

# BETWEEN THE ROCKS

When the giant boulder that squats like an enormous Buddha in the middle of Karen Bussolini's hillside garden split, it left a small, shaded, roomlike space. Within these confines, and aided by rich, moist soil, Karen created a garden that suggests downhill movement. Here the plants are Japanese hakone grass, hardy plumbago, Bowles' golden sedge, fernleaf corydalis, and variegated plectranthus.

### Japanese hakone grass
*Hakonechloa macra*
The idea here is that the Japanese hakone grass, which has a flowing, very directional habit — like water flowing down the mountainside — will suggest movement. The intense yellow, swordlike leaves of Japanese hakone grass vibrate with the blue of the hardy plumbago. *Hakonechloa macra* is the straight species, taller than 'Aureola' and other cultivars. Hardy to Zone 5. 16"–18" tall × 16" wide.

### Bowles' golden sedge
*Carex elata* 'Aurea'
Characterized by compact clumps of deep yellow, arching leaves. This grass repeats the yellow-blue color theme of the hardy plumbago and Japanese hakone grass. Hardy to Zone 5. 28" tall × 18" wide.

### Hardy plumbago
*Ceratostigma plumbaginoides*
The hardy plumbago featured here comes up late, covering spring bulbs, and tucking itself into cracks. A creeping perennial with intense blue flowers that come on in late summer and fall and a tendency to work its way between rocks, hardy plumbago is perfect for the shady floor of this planting. Hardy to Zone 5. 18" tall × 12" wide.

### Fernleaf corydalis
*Corydalis cheilanthifolia*
This fernlike perennial bears bright yellow flowers from spring through summer and self-sows all over the place, including into invisible cracks in the boulder. Karen practices "gardening by subtraction" and removes it only where she doesn't want it. Hardy to Zone 5. 12" tall × 10" wide.

### Variegated plectranthus
*Plectranthus forsteri* 'Marginatus'
Although tender, variegated plectranthus fills in fast, and its bold leaves contrast beautifully with the finer textured fernleaf corydalis. The fast-growing plant will fill out in just a few months of warm weather, and its large leaves with creamy margins are sure to draw attention. Hardy to Zone 13; overwinter indoors in most climates. 10" tall × 3' wide.

---

*designer tips*

## Making More Plectranthus

One of the easiest plants to propagate variegated plectranthus roots easily in a cup of water. Take three- to four-inch-long tip cuttings and strip off the lower leaves. Stick them in water. When they are kept warm, cuttings will root in two to three weeks. You can also divide a larger plant into several smaller plants.

# PERFECT GROUND COVER COLOR

Running along the edge of a gravel path, this trio of low growers forms intertwining mounds of unexpected color. While purple-blue and white are seen together often enough, the addition of orange in the form of a 'Ben More' rockrose livens up the party considerably. The purple-blue, orange, and white work perfectly together along this xeric pathside planting by designer Greg Foreman. This planting, which Foreman has mulched with gravel, is not coincidentally an excellent grouping for rock gardens.

*'Ben More' rockrose livens up the party.*

### 'Ben More' rock rose
*Helianthemum nummularium 'Ben More'*
The deep orange flowers with little, bright yellow eyes make this rock rose easy to recommend — it's like a little mound of tangerine power in the garden. In addition to the plants featured in this set, 'Ben More' is excellent when paired with lavenders. Like lavender, rockroses enjoy full sun and well-drained soils. Hardy to Zone 5. 4" tall × 15" wide.

### 'Druett's Variegated' campion
*Silene uniflora 'Druett's Variegated'*
This little campion puts on a matinee performance in spring with its numerous little balloon-shaped flowers. Out of bloom, its variegated leaves, which are edged in creamy white, continue the interest. A good plant to let cascade over rocks or low walls. Hardy to Zone 4. 2"–4" tall × 8"–12" wide.

### Upside-down sage
*Salvia jurisicii*
A great, true blue, eastern European sage, upside-down sage puts on a conspicuous show of inverted flowers along its upright spikes late in spring. Tolerant of many soil types, upside-down sage should be planted in full sun. Hardy to Zone 4. 12" tall × 12"–15" wide.

*designer tips*

## Time Your Blooms

Bloom timing is key when making garden beds that rely on flowers for interest. In this combination, Greg Foreman planned for the campion to bloom first, but just as it begins going out of bloom, he has upside-down sage and rockrose coming into full flower.

# MOUNDS FOR COVERING GROUNDS

For low care and year-round interest, a mix of evergreen shrubs, ornamental grasses, and creeping sedums — laid out in ribbonlike swathes — is hard to top. This cast of tough and durable plants is also effective because of its use of foliage color — from deep pine green to blue-silver to lime-green with red accents. Although none of these plants have particularly notable blooms, they really don't need them. The strong foliage colors stand on their own.

## Plant in Stripes

For a clean, modernist look, plant three species, low to high, in uniform stripes, as shown here. For an interesting silver, green, and burgundy look in summer, plant stripes of 'Silver Falls' dichondra (*Dichondra argentea* 'Silver Falls'), gulf muhly (*Muhlenbergia capillaris*), and Summer Wine ninebark (*Physocarpus opulifolius* 'Seward').

### Dwarf mugo pine
*Pinus mugo var. mugo*
A standard landscape plant across much of the country, the mugo pine stands up to all manner of use and abuse. Its handsome, dark green needles grow slowly, and the pine's habit varies from rounded (as seen here) to broadly spreading. Hardy to Zone 3. 5'–10' tall × 5'–15' wide.

### 'Elijah Blue' fescue
*Festuca glauca* 'Elijah Blue'
One of the bluest and best of the fescues, 'Elijah Blue' is grown mostly for its symmetrical sea urchin–like mounds. Its arching seed heads are also pretty. Plant in full sun for best blue coloration. Hardy to Zone 4. 6"–14" tall × 6"–8" wide.

### 'Silverine' hens and chicks
*Sempervivum tectorum* 'Silverine'
Noted for the way their offsets (babies) cluster around the mother plant, these low-growing, mat-forming, rosette-shaped succulents make a great ground cover in fast-draining soils or in rock gardens. Although the rosettes die after blooming and setting seed, the offsets carry on in their stead. 'Silverine', as its name suggests, is noted for silver-blue leaves that are tinged with pink. Full sun, or part shade in hot climates. Hardy to Zone 5. 3"–6" tall × 1'–2' wide.

*Although none of these plants have notable blooms, they don't need them; the strong foliage colors stand on their own.*

# TURKISH-AFRICAN GROUND COVER FUSION

Panayoti Kelaidis, internationally known plantsman and a director at Denver Botanic Gardens, calls Turkish speedwell and hardy yellow ice plant "the second most popular ground covers in Denver, just behind grass." Made up of exceptional ground covers for the entire Intermountain West, this electric yellow and blue duo thrives in moderately fertile, well-drained soils. In hot, arid climates both ground covers appreciate afternoon shade.

*A thick mat of succulent foliage with plump leaves that resemble baby toes*

### Turkish speedwell
*Veronica liwanensis*
A 1997 Colorado Plant Select winner, Turkish speedwell has crept across Rocky Mountain gardening culture like a sky-blue tide. Because it is low growing, with attractive deep green, evergreen leaves, and because in Denver it can be grown without irrigation, this speedwell has become a standard planting. In early spring, its numerous flower spikes make a carpet of blue that corresponds perfectly to the bloom time of hardy yellow ice plant. Hardy to Zone 4. 2" tall × 18" wide.

### Hardy yellow ice plant
*Delosperma nubigenum*
This ice plant forms a thick mat of succulent foliage with plump, bright green leaves that resemble baby toes. In the early spring, it will light up with bright yellow flowers. This South African native is drought tolerant, but it will need a bit more supplemental water than Turkish speedwell. Panayoti Kelaidis recommends providing it with afternoon shade in hot climates such as that of Albuquerque. Hardy to Zone 5. 2" tall × 3' wide.

## designer tips

## Grass Alternatives and Living Mulches

Ground covers like Turkish speedwell and hardy yellow ice plant are great grass substitutes and can be used as a living mulch to reduce soil temperatures and suppress weeds. When planting these perennial ground covers, place them three inches closer together than their mature widths to ensure full coverage. In addition to Turkish speedwell and hardy ice plant, try 'Cascade Purple' rock cress (*Aubrieta* × 'Cascade Purple') or 'Pink Chintz' creeping thyme (*Thymus serpyllum* 'Pink Chintz').

# Perennial Rumble on the Hell-strip

When you want to find the toughest plants for your area, you often don't have to look farther than public landscapes. In this duo, 'Homestead Purple' verbena and wine cups form "a sizzling combo from mid-May on," says Lenny Wilson of the Delaware Center for Horticulture. In fact, Wilson remarks that this hell-strip (the area between the curb and sidewalk) planting "is a site similar to many of the public landscapes we nurture [in Wilmington, Delaware]. They are often next to streets, where they have to survive lots of reflected heat." What makes this collection stand out is the vigor and vibrancy of the tough purple and magenta plants duking it out for territory, a fight that spills out right onto the blacktop.

*designer tips*

## Back Up Your Purples with Blues and Whites

Back up these bright-colored, purple ground covers with more restrained colors. Wilson likes to plant *Amsonia* 'Blue Ice' and *Rosa* 'White Drift' behind the 'Homestead Purple' and wine cups. These provide a cool, icy white background to the magenta and purples of the verbena and poppy mallow.

### 'Homestead Purple' verbena
*Verbena canadensis* 'Homestead Purple'

'Homestead Purple' is the hardiest of all the verbenas, one that often survives winters that it's not supposed to. As Wilson says, "'Homestead Purple' is not supposed to be hardy here, but has successfully overwintered for five years." Not only is it hardy, but also it has extraordinarily large, deep-purple flowers. This is an exceptionally rich-colored and long-blooming ground cover. It will tolerate heat, humidity, and clay soils. Cut it back in mid-July to revive it for strong rebloom by September. Cut it back a final time in early winter, and mulch with fallen leaves in cold climates for added protection. Hardy to Zone 7. 6"–10" tall × 3' wide.

### Wine cups
*Callirhoe involucrata*

Showy, heat- and drought-tolerant, and not picky about soil, this plant is born for adversity. Plant it on hot south- or west-facing strips or let it cascade over masonry walls and it will not disappoint. The five-petaled, cup-shaped, fuchsia-colored flowers begin in summer and don't slow down until cold weather arrives. It will reseed if you let it, but not in an annoying way. Cut back wine cups in mid-July to encourage a strong rebloom by September. Hardy to Zone 4. 5" tall × 24"–30" wide.

Tough purple and magenta plants duking it out for territory

# DUTCH MINIMALISM IN NEW YORK

On the southerly tip of Manhattan, beneath a shady canopy of sycamore trees, Dutch designer Piet Oudolf has woven a rich tapestry of plantings characteristic of his fluid and natural design work. This uniquely metropolitan garden adjacent to the Staten Island ferry terminal is in the most urban of situations; while I was photographing it, I had to remove a cardboard box that appeared to have been used as bedding the previous night. In this combination, two vastly different plants (in terms of their texture and color) run up hard against each other. Although the plants look so different, their culture is almost identical. Both like moist, fertile soil in an open location with partial shade — perfect for their situation under the sycamores.

## designer tips

## Favorites for Moist, Partial Shade

In addition to the two ground covers listed here, Oudolf often uses the following plants in moist, part-sun locations. Try Virginia bluebells (*Mertensia virginica*), purple lance astilbe (*Astilbe chinensis* var. *taquetii* 'Purpurlanze' ['Purple Lance']), swamp milkweed (*Asclepias incarnata*), and toad lily (*Tricyrtis formosana*).

**Palm sedge**
*Carex muskingumensis*
The sculptural, chartreuse blades of this grass go a long way toward making this fusion appealing. The architectural pattern of its leaves contrasts nicely with the dark foliage of its planting partner. Moist, fertile soil; sun or part shade. Zone 3. 2"–3" tall × 2"–3" wide.

**'Hot Lips' turtlehead**
*Chelone lyonii* 'Hot Lips'
With foliage so green it tends toward black, 'Hot Lips' is one of those cool native plants that makes you wonder why it isn't planted everywhere. Like the palm branch sedge, it prefers rich, moist soil. It gets its genus name, *Chelone*, from the Greek nymph who was turned into a turtle for not attending the wedding of Zeus and Hera. Hardy to Zone 4. 2'–3' tall × 1' wide.

*Two vastly different plants run up hard against each other.*

# SUCCULENTS FOR EXTREME TEXTURE

Just two plants, both reliable spreading succulents, form a luxurious (if spiny) carpet in a formal planting bed at Longwood Gardens — a place where you might not expect to find a prickly pear snuggled up with a sedum. This planting — a style that is perhaps best described as extreme texture — demonstrates just how powerful differing textures and plant colors can be.

## Prickly Plants and Easements

Landscape designers sometimes advise homeowners against planting thorny plants next to walkways. At face value, this makes sense, but there are many small and astonishing cactus that are best observed at close range and will not poke the casual observer. Unless your friends are lawyers or are unusually clumsy, a pair of agaves framing an entryway, for example, is one of the most conspicuous methods of letting visitors know where to approach a doorway. The trick is to allow enough room for the prickly plant to reach its mature size (and particularly its width) without encroaching on your pathways or other easements.

**Sprawling prickly pear**
*Opuntia phaeacantha*
The low, ground-hugging shape of this prickly pear marks it as a good species for cold climates. Its paddle-shaped, spiky pads offer a stark contrast to the billowy clouds of sedum blooms nearby. The yellow flowers mature into upright fruit that turn pink then burgundy. Hardy to Zone 5. 12"–48" tall × 24"–48" wide.

**'Autumn Joy' sedum**
*Sedum 'Autumn Joy'*
With bright green leaves and budded flower heads that look a little like broccoli florets, this showy sedum is hard not to love. In early autumn, it produces flat umbels of deep pink flowers, which mature to coppery brown, providing a long season of interest. The deep pink blossoms look especially fine in relation to the olive-colored pads of the prickly pear. Hardy to Zone 3. 2' × 2' wide.

*This planting shows just how powerful differing textures can be.*

# BUDDIES FOR
## Woodies

Although trees and shrubs often take a back-seat to flashier perennials, their importance in the landscape is a primary concern. Woody plants — trees and shrubs with stiff and, well, woody, rather than soft herbaceous stems — are often passed over by gardeners greedy for the space that trees take away from other plantings. While it's true that planting beneath large trees can be a challenge, trees and rugged shrubs provide the largest benefits with the lowest maintenance requirements of any plant category. They truly are the draft horses of our gardens.

Nearly all designers begin planning a garden by placing the trees and large shrubs first. They are the bones of the design, and the location, height, spread, and color of woody plants drive what goes where in the rest of the landscape. Even perennial proponents Piet Oudolf and Noel Kingsbury concede, "Perennial plants need a context, for which woody plants are essential."

The trees and shrubs featured in this section are not the simplified green lollypops that you drew in grade school. They are mostly small- to medium-size specimens that fit within the confines of small contemporary gardens. Many exhibit unusual branching structure and leaf color — silver, burgundy, gold, and chartreuse — to provide a vibrant backdrop for other plants. Because designers are often the first to get their hands on new cultivars, exciting new trees like 'Hearts of Gold' redbuds show up here, along with threatened, longtime favorites like American elm. All and all, the combinations with woody plants show precisely why trees and shrubs should be used: because they integrate so well with lower-growing plants.

With the shrinking size of many American gardens, selecting trees that won't overwhelm a garden has become increasingly important, and a bounty of new dwarf trees and shrubs have been developed to meet the challenge. Several of these compact woodies are highlighted in this chapter.

*Sambucus racemosa* 'Sutherland Gold' lights up this textural combination with *Artemisia* 'Powis Castle', the strappy foliage of an ornamental grass, and an allium seed head, at Colonial Park in Somerset, New Jersey.

# Gathered Around a Smart Young Lady

With the popularity of the dark-colored smoke tree (featured in several combinations in this book), it is refreshing to see 'Young Lady', a small, mauve-colored cultivar, tucked so smartly into a bed of pink-flowered annuals and perennials. The design, conceived by former Chicago Botanic Gardens horticulturist Catharine Mann, adds vertical notes through a combination of 'Camelot Rose' foxglove and drumstick allium. The pink, flouncy flowers of 'Silver Cup' mallow add a feminine touch that corresponds with the soft pink plumes of 'Young Lady' smoke tree. Although this combination is planted at Chicago Botanic Gardens, it could be applied easily in a home garden flanking an entryway or announcing the beginning of a path.

### 'Young Lady' smoke tree
*Cotinus coggygria* 'Young Lady'
An import from Holland, 'Young Lady' is unusual among smoke tree cultivars in that it blooms profusely even as a very young plant. Frothy, pink panicles emerge above the blue-green, oval leaves from June through August. It is also smaller than other smoke trees and can be grown well in a container, where it will pose like a well-groomed poodle. In fall, its foliage turns yellow, orange, and red. As used here, it makes a nicely behaved focal point among showy pink perennials and annuals. Hardy to Zone 4. 8'–10' tall × 8'–10' wide.

### 'Camelot Rose' foxglove
*Digitalis purpurea* 'Camelot Rose'
This hybrid foxglove, whose flowers are a combination of deep rose, white, and cream colors, has been bred to take more sun than other foxgloves. In late spring to early summer, 'Camelot' sends up a four-foot flower spike that persists on the plant for some time. (This photo was taken in mid-July, past peak bloom, but still interesting.) Good soil, ample water, and afternoon shade are preferable for most foxgloves. Hardy to Zone 4. 42"–48" tall × 24"–30" wide.

### 'Silver Cup' mallow
*Lavatera trimestris* 'Silver Cup'
A dwarf, bushy Mediterranean mallow with vibrant pink, four-inch flowers and attractive, mid-green, fuzzy foliage is very showy through the summer and early fall and flowers at a time when other plants are often out of bloom. 'Silver Cup' is a stout variety that doesn't require staking. Prefers full sun and ordinary soil. Sow seeds indoors in late winter or early spring and set out plants after all danger of frost has passed. Annual. 18"–30" tall × 18" wide.

### 'Coronation Gold' yarrow
*Achillea filipendulina* 'Coronation Gold'
When is comes to yarrows, 'Coronation Gold' is simply the best. Yarrows have a somewhat well-earned reputation as garden thugs for their proclivity to reseed where you don't want them. 'Coronation Gold', which is sterile, is a breed apart from common yarrow and stays put. It's also a strong rebloomer with delicate foliage and intensely gold flowers. Unlike taller, seed-grown varieties, 'Coronation Gold' won't crowd out its smaller neighbors. And unlike the popular variety 'Moonshine', the flowers of 'Coronation Gold' are anything but muted. In fact, the term "screaming yellow" comes to mind. Hardy to Zone 3. 36" tall × 24" wide.

### Drumstick allium
*Allium sphaerocephalum*
As its common name suggests, this allium has bell-shaped ornamental heads of deep pink flowers with oniony green foliage. Wonderfully architectural and vertical, drumstick allium stands out, especially when mixed with soft leafy plants, as it is here. Hardy to Zone 4. 20"–36" tall × 12" wide.

# INSPIRED CALLIGRAPHY

Just three plants combine for early autumn impact in this bold arrangement. Creeping into the vignette, the 'Autumn Spire' provides a dash of red, like a confident brushstroke in black and red Japanese calligraphy. The dwarf purple willow, a fixture in Duncan Brine's garden, serves as a fine-textured pillow for the bolder 'Tardiva' hydrangea and red fall leaves of the 'Autumn Spire' maple. In this display, the familiar safety of an organized foreground leading to distant background has been pulled away. As Brine says, "The garden guest comes face to face with looming shrubs. Distant views and plant variety suddenly diminish, and all that's left is the relationship between the guest and the three large shrubs."

## Divine Provenance: Choose Your *Acer rubrum* Well

Because *Acer rubrum* is native from Canada to Florida, cold hardiness varies considerably based on the tree's provenance (where the species evolved and grows naturally). For this reason, provenance becomes important when selecting a tree. While 'Autumn Spire' may be ideal for northern gardeners, it may suffer in southern heat. For the best performance, choose a tree with provenance as close as possible to your planting location.

### 'Nana' dwarf purple willow

*Salix purpurea* 'Nana'

The mass of the dwarf willow provides textural contrast for the differing leaf color, size, and shape of the hydrangea. Forming the edge of a maze in this combination, the willow is truly a sculptural element in Brine's garden. Hardy to Zone 4. 3' tall × 5' wide.

### 'Autumn Spire' maple

*Acer rubrum* 'Autumn Spire'

This University of Minnesota introduction is noted for its blazing red, early fall color; cold hardiness; and columnar shape. Its deeply lobed leaves begin turning vivid red as early as late August in Brine's New York garden. Grow in moist, well-drained soils that tend toward the acid side of the pH scale. Hardy to Zone 3. 50' tall × 20'–25' wide.

### 'Tardiva' hydrangea

*Hydrangea paniculata* 'Tardiva'

A late-blooming hydrangea, 'Tardiva' is an excellent choice for planting beneath large, open, shade trees, although it will grow in full sun as well. Its coarse leaves and sizable panicles of pink-tinged white flowers generate a lot of interest. Its flowers form on new wood, so the plant benefits greatly from a spring pruning. Hardy to Zone 4. 6'–8' tall × 8'–10' wide

*'Autumn Spire' provides a dash of red, like a confident stroke in black and red Japanese calligraphy.*

# WILDLY TAMED

Designer Marcia Tatroe has no qualms about situating a wild and woolly shrub like silver fountain butterfly bush right next to a cultured gent like 'Gold Cone' juniper; in fact, as she demonstrates here, both plants are better for the association. This look is part of a design strategy that Tatroe describes as the beauty of "vastly dissimilar leaves" in which the designer uses highly varied textures and colors (read: orange and purple) to excite the eye.

## designer tips

### Pruning Your Silver Fountain Butterfly Bush

When you have a flashy and unusual shrub like silver fountain butterfly bush, you want to take care to keep it in prime shape. For silver fountain butterfly bush, that means waiting to cut it back until after it's bloomed. Unlike some other butterfly bushes (especially the *Buddleia davidii* cultivars), which are cut back hard each spring to promote new growth, silver fountain butterfly bush blooms on last year's growth; therefore, you need wait to shape it until after it blooms in early summer.

### Silver fountain butterfly bush
*Buddleia alternifolia* 'Argentea'
Large and superbly rangy, silver fountain butterfly bush bears its lavender-purple flowers in spiral fashion along branches that reach out like wild tentacles over surrounding plants. Silver fountain butterfly bush can be pruned as a small tree, but its best purpose is to be used as the centerpiece of a naturalistic planting, as shown here. Hardy to Zone 4. 12'–15' tall × 10'–12' wide.

### 'Gold Cone' juniper
*Juniperus communis* 'Gold Cone'
This compact and uniform cone-shaped juniper with golden new foliage provides the perfect formal yellow contrast to the wild and wandlike branches of the silver fountain butterfly bush. Full sun. Hardy to Zone 5. 3'–5' tall × 1'–2' wide.

### 'Melton Pastels' pincushion plant
*Knautia macedonica* 'Melton Pastels'
This perennial pincushion relative produces pink, mauve, red, blue, and salmon blossoms on long, wiry stems. Avoid soggy soils and give it full sun to part shade. Hardy to Zone 5. 20" tall × 12" wide.

### Sea thrift
*Armeria pseudarmeria*
Its pale pink flower heads on onionlike stems resemble drumsticks and add verticality and architecture to the middle of the border. Hardy to Zone 5. 20" tall × 12" wide.

### Soapwort
*Saponaria ocymoides*
Growing beneath the pincushion plant, soapwort provides an enchanting and dense pink ground cover that is sure to have garden visitors asking for seeds. Soapwort reseeds itself vigorously, but a timely shearing as the flowers fade will prevent reseeding and improve the plant's post-flowering looks. Hardy to Zone 3. 10" tall × 24" wide.

### Yellow-horned poppy
*Glaucium flavum*
Growing from a silvery rosette, yellow-horned poppy flowers emerge either yellow or orange on stiff stems. The orange flowers are the perfect counterpoint to the lavender blooms of silver fountain butterfly bush. This poppy is a short-lived perennial usually grown as a biennial. Hardy to Zone 6. 12"–36" tall × 18" wide.

# GATHERED AROUND THE 'BONFIRE'

When designer Inta Krombolz combines hot colors, she does it with an exclamation point (!) or three (!!!) in the form of three dark red or nearly black 'Helmond Pillar' Japanese barberries, which blast skyward out of a sea of burgundy and orange. As exceptional as the barberry column is, it is not the true star of this design. That distinction goes to the 'Bonfire' dwarf peach whose unusual, dark burgundy-blue weeping leaves command attention. Firing things up in the foreground, Krombolz uses 'Louie's Orange Delight' sage and another exclamation point, this time in the form of a chartreuse fastigiate, Japanese plum yew.

*A nearly black 'Helmond Pillar' barberry blasts skyward out of a sea of burgundy and orange.*

### Japanese hakone grass
*Hakonechloa macra*
The idea here is that the Japanese hakone grass, which has a flowing, very directional habit — like water flowing down the mountainside — will suggest movement. The intense yellow, swordlike leaves of Japanese hakone grass vibrate with the blue of the hardy plumbago. *Hakonechloa macra* is the straight species, taller than 'Aureola' and other cultivars. Hardy to Zone 5. 16"–18" tall × 16" wide.

### 'Helmond Pillar' Japanese barberry
*Berberis thunbergii* 'Helmond Pillar'
As you can see, this is an excellent vertical accent, especially when its color is echoed in surrounding plants, as it is here. This super adaptable plant tolerates polluted urban areas and drought. For best (deepest purple) foliage, plant in full sun. It dislikes soggy soils. Hardy to Zone 4. 4'–5' × 1'–2' wide.

### 'Bonfire' dwarf peach
*Prunus persica* 'Bonfire'
This great little peach with lustrous, dark burgundy-blue leaves bears double, pink flowers in spring. This peach bears inedible fruit, which are usually hidden by the big drooping leaves. The pits will often sprout into young trees beneath the mother plant. Likes good, moist soil, slightly on the acid side. Hardy to Zone 5. 4'–7' tall × 4'–7' wide.

### 'Louie's Orange Delight' sage
*Salvia splendens* 'Louie's Orange Delight'
This vivid salvia brings some tropical heat front and center in this ensemble. In hot climates, 'Louie's Orange Delight' prefers afternoon shade. Hardy to Zone 9. 3' tall × 3' wide.

### Fastigiate Japanese plum yew
*Cephalotaxus harringtonia* 'Fastigiata'
Lustrous foliage, tinged with yellow and very slow growing, characterizes this deer-resistant plant. Female plum yews produce clusters of small, fleshy, plumlike fruit. Tolerant of pruning. Hardy to Zone 6. 10' tall × 6'–8' wide.

## designer tips

## Fight Fire with Fire
Although at first glance her designs might appear to be a riot of color, the colors Inta Krombolz chooses are selected with a single-minded vision. As she explains, "I like to use hot colors together, and I don't mix cool and hot colors. For example, I won't put blue or white in a garden that has oranges, reds, or burgundies. I like to create interest with colors that vary in tone but don't contrast too much."

# BENEATH BIRCHES

If you're going to simplify your combinations, you need special plants arranged just so. This goal is what designer Julie Siegel realizes in this twosome of 'Royal Frost' birch underplanted with a minor sea of vivid palm sedge. The dark purple leaves of the birch weeping over the bright yellow-green palm sedge evoke a wild woodland theme. It should be noted that both plants like moist, fertile soil and are thus well matched horticulturally as well as aesthetically. Both plants also provide a long season of interest — even over winter, when the birch becomes a stark sculpture of white and purple and the palm sedge turns into tawny little haystacks in the snow.

## designer tips

### Consider Your Background

When you're planting in front of a house or garden walls, consider the color of your background. In this planting, Julie Siegel selected the 'Royal Frost' birch purposely to contrast with the white modern stucco house in the background. In the winter, the white walls of the house set off the dark branches; in spring, the newly emerging purple leaves stand out against the light-colored stucco. Had the house been a dark red brick, the leaves and branches of 'Royal Frost' would be lost.

**'Royal Frost' birch**
*Betula pendula* 'Royal Frost'
Lustrous, purple-tinged foliage and purple twigs contrast with peeling, white-and-copper bark. Leaves turn bronze-green or coppery orange in fall. Unlike some recent purple-leafed introductions, 'Royal Frost' is a vigorous grower. Hardy to Zone 4. 30'–40' tall × 15'–20' wide.

**Palm sedge**
*Carex muskingumensis*
The chartreuse, sculptural blades of this Midwest native contribute a lot to the appeal of this planting. The exquisite, arching architectural pattern of its leaves and seed heads make it a good choice for an interesting ground cover. Moist, fertile soil, sun or part shade. Hardy to Zone 3. 2"–3" tall × 2"–3" wide.

*The dark purple leaves of the birch weeping over the bright yellow-green palm sedge evoke a woodland theme.*

# THE GOLDEN PATH

If you look casually at this Brandon Tyson pathside planting, the first thing that hits you is the color gold;
a crescent of gold box honeysuckle and a background of golden locust jump out at you. Look a little closer
and you'll see that Tyson has mixed in a quartet of columnar boxwood to add some upright green. In garden
design, the color yellow has traditionally been used to move people swiftly through an area. But Tyson does
not stop with gold and yellow; he also includes several subtle, small-flowered burgundy- to black-flowering
plants. In the foreground, he introduces an unusual species geranium with gray leaves and then interweaves
a mysterious and sought-after black-flowering Andean silver leaf sage.

Designer Plant Combinations

## Reining in Speedsters

When you plant a fast grower like golden locust, you may want to restrict its growth through aggressive pruning. This practice has the added benefit of encouraging new growth that will be closer to the lower-growing plants you pair with it. Two methods of severe pruning are pollarding and coppicing. When pollarding, you cut back all of the smaller stems to one main stem (this would be to the trunk in trees); when coppicing, you cut everything back to just above ground level. Both of these methods are recommended only for trees in which you want to produce a lot of new shoots and leaves in tighter arrangement than they would be in a traditionally pruned tree. Some plants that are often coppiced are smoke trees (*Cotinus*) and willows (*Salix*).

### Geranium
*Pelargonium sidoides*
If you have geranium fatigue, this is the plant for you; it's nothing like the usual geraniums you see *ad nauseum* in California gardens. Relatively small, hairy, silver leaves and tiny, jewel-like, dark purple flowers (in addition to its compact habit) recommend this species geranium for much wider garden use. Hardy to Zone 9. 12" tall × 12" wide.

### Gold box honeysuckle
*Lonicera nitida* 'Baggesen's Gold'
Lacy, evergold foliage sets this shrubby plant apart. This tough plant can be started from a four-inch pot and can be whacked completely to the ground to come back fresh the next season. Grow in full sun to part shade in well-drained soil. Whether used en masse or singly, this is a plant that will not be ignored. Hardy to Zone 7. 3' tall × 3' wide.

### 'Graham Blandy' boxwood
*Buxus sempervirens* 'Graham Blandy'
This very narrow, columnar boxwood lends some dark green to this arrangement. Highly sought after for its very slow upward growth, 'Graham Blandy' requires very little pruning to keep its columnar form. Hardy to Zone 5. 8'–10' tall × 2' wide.

### Andean silver-leaf sage
*Salvia discolor*
The inimitable, purple-black flowers of Andean silver-leaf sage, which emerge from pistachio-green calyces, are about as close to midnight as you can find. Its silver leaves and sticky stems add to the allure of this collectable Peruvian sage. Here, its silver leaves are a great cool foil for the yellow plants in front and behind. Hardy to Zone 10. 2'–3' tall × 1' wide.

### Iochroma
*Iochroma cyaneum*
This iochroma is a large, tropical shrub with tubular, purple-red flowers, but iochromas in general come in a huge variety and are vastly underutilized in the garden. They are fast growing, easy to prune, and great for hummingbirds. Full sun or partial sun. Hardy to Zone 9. 7'–10' tall × 7'–10' wide.

### 'Frisia' golden locust
*Robinia pseudoacacia* 'Frisia'
The lemon-yellow to chartreuse (if grown in shade) pinnate leaves are the main attraction of the golden locust, and the intensity of the color is matched by few trees. The size of this locust is easily controlled through pruning — it's very fast growing. Unlike a lot of chartreuse plants, 'Frisia' keeps its color all season. Golden locusts, like other members of the genus *Robinia*, sucker freely and, if left unpruned, will make a large, multitrunked shrub. Drought and heat tolerant. Hardy to Zone 4. 50' tall × 25' wide.

# Surfing for Wild Lilacs

When professional landscape designer and amateur surfer Dave Buchanan approaches a garden, he brings with him a head full of California plant dreams. "I grew up playing in the canyons around San Diego, and I learned the plants there. When I plan a garden, I include some of the plants that we are losing to development." When Buchanan pilots his surfboard and nursery container–laden Toyota pickup toward a beach, he's not just looking for waves, he's also scanning the coastal sages and scrub for gardenworthy species. In this coastal hillside garden, Buchanan selects a pair of mountain lilacs, a sunflower, and a shimmering silver sage to provide both beauty and erosion control. Using two strong primary colors — blue and yellow — it's hard to go wrong. On a windy spring afternoon, the blue mountain lilacs even look a little like waves.

## designer tips

### Avoid Plant Pile-Ups

When laying out low-growing or dwarf species and cultivars, Buchanan suggests giving them "sufficient spacing, and have a little patience while they fill in. Planting too close forces horizontal growers to start mounding over one another, causing higher growth heights and a tendency to cause under-canopy branch dieback due to shading out lower foliage." He says, "Interplant the open spaces with wildflowers or perennials that will be showy until ground covers fill in."

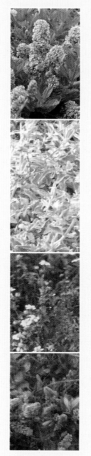

### 'Yankee Point' mountain lilac
*Ceanothus griseus* var. *horizontalis* 'Yankee Point'
Although it's low growing, 'Yankee Point' mountain lilac is a plant that likes to stretch out its legs like an NBA player in a La-Z-Boy recliner. A great plant for stabilizing banks and growing among rocks, this low-growing cultivar can spread to 12 feet in diameter, making a handsome circle of glossy, green leaves and, in spring, a magical show of powder blue flowers. Hardy to Zone 8. 2'–3' tall × 8'–12' wide.

### 'Point Sal' purple sage
*Salvia leucophylla* 'Point Sal'
Extremely fragrant, low-growing 'Point Sal' purple sage provides a high contrast of silver foliage poking out of the surrounding deep green mountain lilacs. Like 'Yankee Point', 'Point Sal' is relatively low growing but vigorously spreading. Like many coastal shrubs, it likes fast drainage and infrequent summer watering after establishment. Hummingbirds patronize its rose-purple flowers. Hardy to Zone 8. 2'–3' tall × 6'–8' wide.

### San Diego sunflower
*Viguiera laciniata*
This classic, southern California wildling is the perfect bushy sunflower to brighten up its cool-flowered companions. With a multitude of bright yellow-orange daisies borne on wiry stems, this sunflower is extremely drought tolerant and blooms from spring to early summer. Hardy to Zone 8. 1'–2' tall × 1'–3' wide.

### 'Ray Hartman' mountain lilac
*Ceanothus* 'Ray Hartman'
'Ray Hartman' is a burly stand-up kind of dude and a perfect background plant in this hillside location. 'Ray Hartman' can even be pruned into a small tree. Here it's a nice bookend to the lower growing 'Point Sal' mountain lilac. Provide good drainage. Hardy to Zone 8. 12'–20' tall × 15'–20' wide.

# PURPLE-PINK WORKHORSES

Woody shrubs and small trees sometimes get passed over for more-colorful, summer-flowering annuals and perennials. Garden designer Stephanie Cohen thinks this is a mistake. With this duo, she employs two tough, woody plants like a pair of handsome draft horses. The plants, a cutleaf lilac and 'Forest Pansy' redbud, provide more screening and seasonal interest than a typical perennial planting would. As captured here, they virtually explode in lilac and fuchsia in spring. Later in the season, the fine, green, cutleaf foliage of the lilac contrasts nicely with the large, heart-shaped, maroon leaves of 'Forest Pansy'.

## designer tips

### Let Your Redbud Dance with Itself

Stephanie Cohen advises gardeners to give redbuds enough space to mature. "This tree is wider than it is high" she says, "Give it space. Poor pruning will give you some kind of truncated tree. Let it dance by itself. You only need to remove suckers and prune out dead wood. The flowering and foliage make it interesting for the entire gardening season — even in winter it has a nice form."

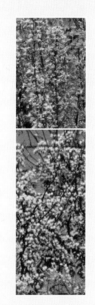

**Cutleaf lilac**
*Syringa × laciniata*
With smaller, more delicate leaves than other lilacs, cutleaf lilac is a more interesting choice as either a specimen or screen than more commonly planted lilac hybrids. Its fragrant flower panicles (flower spikes) are produced in late spring. Hardy to Zone 4. 6' tall × 10' wide.

**'Forest Pansy' redbud**
*Cercis canadensis* 'Forest Pansy'
Its distinctive, dark-hued, purple-red leaves make 'Forest Pansy' one of the most impressive of the redbud tree cultivars. The mutable leaves, which change from purple to green with purple veins in midsummer to yellow in fall, add to the allure. As mentioned above, its big, heart-shaped leaves are a perfect foliar complement to finer textured shrubs. 'Forest Pansy' has graceful ascending branches that make it great for courtyard plantings. Hardy to Zone 4. 20'–30' tall × 25'–35' wide.

'Forest Pansy' redbud and cutleaf lilac are like a pair of handsome draft horses.

# HEARTS OF GOLD

In a bed designed to emphasize a specific color — in this case, yellow and yellow-greens — Jonathan Wright proves that monochromatic color schemes can be as or more exciting and diverse than polychromatic plantings. In this arrangement, which is built around the stunning yellow-green leaves of a 'Hearts of Gold' redbud tree, the plants seem to be lit from within. The mixture provides a glowing mix of foliage and floral pleasures — all on the yellow side of the color wheel.

### 'Hearts of Gold' redbud
*Cercis canadensis* 'Hearts of Gold'
The first gold-leaved hybrid introduced in the United States, 'Hearts of Gold' is sure to be a highly sought-after plant in home gardens. It maintains its leaf color in full sun and blooms lavender-purple flowers in spring, before the foliage emerges. Its leaves are so large and yellow-green that at first glance it resembles a pollarded golden catalpa. Hardy to Zone 5. 15' tall × 18' wide.

### Variegated giant reed grass
*Arundo donax* 'Variegata'
A strong vertical accent with arching, cornlike leaves, variegated giant reed grass is more luminous, compact, and controlled than its nonvariegated brother. Its yellow, white, and green stripes make it a perfect focal point in midsummer. Hardy to Zone 6. 8'–12' tall × 4' wide.

### 'Autumn Minaret' daylily
*Hemerocallis* 'Autumn Minaret'
Forming an undulating little wall of yellow along the border of the bed, these yellow daylilies add flow and repetition to the design. Although it is a reliable old standard, 'Autumn Minaret' is still highly sought after and sometimes hard to track down. An extremely tall and elegant selection, part of its draw is its see-through stems. Hardy to Zone 3. 5' tall × 3' wide.

### Bonanza Gold Japanese barberry
*Berberis thunbergii* 'Bogozam' (Bonanza Gold)
This patented, low-growing selection of Japanese barberry has gold leaves and red fruit. Its normally ornamental foliage turns a riot of orange and red in fall. Hardy to Zone 4. 18" tall × 3' wide.

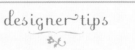

*designer tips*

## When Using One Color, Use Different Textures

Jonathan Wright likens the forms in this planting to "textural play." Because all of the plants display a version of yellow, texture and form become everything. For this reason, when designing a monochromatic area, Wright advises that you use diverse shapes. For example, this planting employs round redbud leaves, arching giant reed grass, and a cloudlike mass of daylily flowers to entertain the eye.

# RED VELVET SMOKE TREE CURTAIN

About this display, Duncan Brine remarks, "Light blue is a subtle yet arresting color partner to the deep maroon-red of the smoke tree." All of the plants in this ensemble are long blooming and sun-loving and well suited to hot, dry gardens. Most are blue and rely on the 'Royal Purple' smoke tree to pop off the background. Because the perennials are all within a low height range, they dramatize the stature of the smoke tree.

## designer tips

### Planting Hardy Shrubs in Fall

From October until Thanksgiving, nearly all hardy shrubs, like the 'Royal Purple' smoke tree mentioned here, can be planted. In fact, it is the best time to plant them. As the late *Washington Post* columnist Henry Mitchell wrote, "Fall — not spring — is the great planting season for woody things . . . but most people like to wait until the spring sunshine inspires them to run about like rabbits through clover." Planting in fall also takes advantage of garden center discounts and helps you avoid the spring crowds.

*Light blue is a subtle yet arresting color partner.*

**'Six Hills Giant' catmint**
*Nepeta × faasenii* 'Six Hills Giant'
This vigorous, highly aromatic, gray-green-leaved perennial grows in very hot, sunny conditions. Throughout the summer months, it bears whorls of lavender-blue flowers that just might be the perfect foil for the maroon leaves of the smoke tree. Hardy to Zone 3. 36" tall × 24" wide.

**'Golden Shower' tickseed**
*Coreopsis verticillata* 'Golden Shower'
The deeper green stems and leaves of this tickseed contrast nicely with the surrounding gray, blue, and maroon. In early summer, golden flowers hover over the foliage of this easy-to-grow perennial that spreads by rhizomes — sometimes more than the gardener wants, so beware! Hardy to Zone 4. 24" tall × 18" wide.

**Russian sage**
*Perovskia atriplicifolia*
A workhorse in the hot, dry garden, the lavender-like blooms of Russian sage are a welcome late-summer and fall treat. The interesting white stems and deeply cut leaves add interest to the plant even when it's out of bloom. Tolerates heat and poor, alkaline soils. Hardy to Zone 6. 4' tall × 3' wide.

**'Royal Purple' smoke tree**
*Cotinus coggygria* 'Royal Purple'
Like a velvet theater curtain, royal purple smoke tree is the backdrop for all of the blues, grays, and yellows in this collection: without it, the other plants would be less compelling, and with the smoke tree in back, the colors in front pop. The oval leaves are red-purple turning to scarlet in autumn. The plumelike panicles, which produce a smokelike effect in summer, give the plant its common name. Hardy to Zone 5. 15' tall × 15' wide.

The flame-colored new leaves of mountain laurel (*Kalmia latifolia*) glow among the airy, lavender flower sprays of Siberian bugloss (*Brunnera macrophylla*) in this planting at Ballymore Gardens in Ambler, Pennsylania.

# PURE WHITE LIGHT

It takes a lot of conviction to choose a white theme and stick with it; as Longwood Gardens horticulturist Lauren Goldstein explains, "There is always the temptation to add other colors, but I get picky about keeping the border white. Within the realm of cream, silver, and white, there is a lot to choose from, and by varying the forms we keep it exciting." Lest you think that her white combination is as proper as a Victorian wedding dress, Goldstein supplies a few wild surprises to keep you on your toes. A precocious angel's trumpet muscles its way up through the mid-border, sticking up its funnel-shaped flowers here and there, while clumps of Abyssinian sword lilies knife their way up out of a patch of silver spurflower.

## designer tips

### Rotate Annuals

At Longwood Gardens, perennials are used as the backbone of plantings while annual flowers are rotated out every three months to provide high color impact. Home gardeners can achieve similar effects with a slightly less rigorous schedule. If lots of color is your aim, devote a small and easily accessible area of your garden (perhaps near the front) to annuals and change them out with the seasons. This practice will keep things interesting and let you experiment with all of the new annuals that breeders keep cranking out. Keeping the area small also allows ample room for longer-lived and lower-maintenance plants like perennials and woodies.

*Abyssinian sword lilies knife their way up out of a patch of silver spurflower.*

### Silver spurflower
*Plectranthus argentatus*

Not an annual for the faint of heart, the robust silver spurflower produces shimmering, hairy foliage at a good clip over the summer months. Although it produces spikes of pale blue flowers, silver spurflower's main attributes are its downy, scalloped leaves. Hardy to Zone 10; grown as an annual elsewhere. 34"–36" tall × 18" wide.

### 'Morning Light' maiden grass
*Miscanthus sinensis* 'Morning Light'

'Morning Light' punctuates the foreground with its white and green ribbonlike foliage. In fall, it produces coppery, tassel-like flower stalks that turn wheat colored in winter and persist for good winter interest. A great, wild-looking accent plant, it breaks up large sweeping plantings with something more upright and exciting. Hardy to Zone 5. 4'–6' tall × 2.5'–4' wide.

### Angel's trumpet
*Datura meteloides*

Angel's trumpet loves heat and looks its best in warm, moist soil. In contrast to its close relative, brugmansia (also called angel's trumpet), this angel's trumpet bears its flowers upright rather than dangling down. All parts of the plant are poisonous, so keep it away from youngsters. Hardy to Zone 9; grown as an annual elsewhere. 2'–4' tall × 3'–6' wide.

### Abyssinian sword lily
*Acidanthera bicolor*

An old heirloom gladiolus from 1896, this east African native has strongly scented, pure white flowers with purple markings in their throats. Formerly called *Gladiolus callianthus* 'Murielae', this bulb (corm, actually) likes full sun and well-drained soils. Extremely upright, handsome foliage. Hardy to Zone 7. 28"–39" tall × 12" wide.

### 'Unique' hydrangea
*Hydrangea paniculata* 'Unique'

With a name like 'Unique', you expect something special; in this case, you get a hydrangea with distinctive cream-colored flower heads that are very broad at the base and blunt at the tip. The naturalistic, arching form of 'Unique' requires little pruning, although it can be shaped to fit in small spaces. Moist soil and part shade are best for this hydrangea. Hardy to Zone 5. 10' tall × 8' wide.

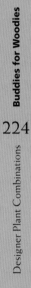
A magenta rose (*Rosa* 'Flower Carpet') shines among swaths of catmint (*Nepeta* × *faassenii*), 'Powis Castle' sage (*Artemisia* × 'Powis Castle'), 'Primrose Heron' lamb's ears (*Stachys* 'Primrose Heron'), and a dwarf agapanthus (*Agapanthus* sp.) in this Freeland Tanner design.

# RACY RED RIOT

Exhibiting color fearlessness, designer and painter Lynden Miller flexes her foliage muscle in this composition of Merlot reds and tree frog yellow-greens. The result is a vignette that has little need for flowers. Miller begins with a central, purple-leaved sand cherry and then recruits other burgundy plants, like Japanese blood grass, down near the front of the border. The zing in this ensemble is provided by the Mellow Yellow spirea in the middle of the border, which glows chartreuse against the red background.

## designer tips

### Label Your Plants

There is nothing more embarrassing than getting stumped by friends visiting your garden who ask, "What is that gorgeous thing?" To stay sharp, do what all the plant gurus do — write the plant name on a plant tag. Plantsman Tony Avent recommends using oil-based markers to label your plants. They will not fade in the sun or wash away, something that cannot be said for regular markers. Other plantspeople swear by pencil, which, remarkably, seems to hold up better than any kind of ink.

### Purple-leaved sand cherry
*Prunus × cistena*
This upright deciduous shrub provides a dynamic hunk of burgundy in this grouping. In midspring, purple-leaved sand cherry blooms pinkish white. Hardy to Zone 3. 7'–10' tall × 5' wide.

### Variegated redtwig dogwood
*Cornus alba* 'Elegantissima'
The only plant in this assemblage with more restrained coloration, variegated redtwig dogwood has gray-green leaves with creamy white margins. A true four-season plant, variegated redtwig dogwood is equally pretty with its red canes displayed in winter. Like other dogwoods, moist to wet soil is a must. Hardy to Zone 2. 10' tall ×10 ' wide.

### False dracaena
*Cordyline* 'Purple Tower'
'Purple Tower' is positioned here directly in front of the screaming yellow-green spirea. For those who enjoy growing hardy tropicals, cordylines take more cold than one might suspect, although they will stay much smaller in colder climates than they do in frost-free zones. Hardy to Zone 8 (and the warmer parts of Zone 7, with protection). 48" tall × 48" wide.

### Mellow Yellow spirea
*Spiraea thunbergii* 'Ogon' (Mellow Yellow)
This spirea begins with mellow, yellow leaves in spring and early summer, which mature into the brilliantly chartreuse leaves pictured here, followed by russet-colored fall foliage. Hardy to Zone 4. Full sun to light shade. 3'–5' tall × 3'–5' wide.

### Japanese blood grass
*Imperata cylindrica* 'Rubra'
With their brilliant red tips, Japanese blood grass spreads out like a wild carpet. The loosely organized clumps enjoy moist soil and full sun. Hardy to Zone 5. 16" tall × 12" wide.

### Balloon flower
*Platycodon grandiflorus*
Although not yet in bloom in this photo, balloon flower's bright green, globe shape makes for good form in the middle of the cluster. Its well-known, purple-blue flowers bloom in mid- to late summer. Plant in moist, well-drained soil. Hardy to Zone 4. 24" tall × 12" wide.

# DESIGNER RESOURCES

**Dan Benarcik**
Chanticleer: A Pleasure
Garden
Wayne, PA
610-688-2919
*www.chanticleergarden.org*

**Julia Berman Design**
Santa Fe, NM
505-820-3314

**Duncan Brine**
Horticultural Design
Pawling, NY
845-855-9023
*horticulturaldesign@
compuserve.com*

**Dave Buchanan**
Ocean Sage Landscaping
Encinitas, CA
760-942-9254
*oceansage@cox.net*

**Karen Bussolini**
Karen Bussolini Photography
South Kent, CT
860-927-4122
*www.agpix.com/
karenbussolini*

**Scott Calhoun**
Zona Gardens
Tucson, AZ
520-867-8038
*www.zonagardens.com*

**Stephanie Cohen**
Collegeville, PA
610-409-8232

**David Cristiani**
The Quercus Group
Albuquerque, NM
505-275-7296
*www.thequercusgroup.com*

**Lisa Delplace**
Oehme, van Sweden
Associates
Washington, DC
202-546-7575
*www.ovsla.com*

**Janet Draper**
Smithsonian Institution
Washington, DC
202-633-2223
*drapeja@si.edu*

**Neil Diboll**
Prairie Nursery
Westfield, WI
800-476-9453
*www.prairienursery.com*

**Greg Foreman**
Natives Among Us
Evergreen, CO
*peaklight@msn.com*

**Joe Henderson**
Chanticleer: A Pleasure
Garden
Wayne, PA
610-688-2919
*www.chanticleergarden.org*

**Panayoti Kelaidis**
Denver Botanic Gardens
Denver, CO
720-865-3500
*www.bontanicgardens.org*

**Inta Krombolz**
Of Fox Hollow
West Chester, PA

**Carrie Nimmer**
Phoenix, AZ
602-758-7001
*queenagave@cox.net*

**Piet Oudolf**
*www.oudolf.com*

**Judith Phillips**
Judith Phillips' Design Oasis
Albuquerque, NM
505-343-1800
*judphil@nmia.com*

**Scott Rothenberger**
Barto, PA
610-428-1801
*gardendesign_SR@
entermail.net*

**David Salman**
High Country Gardens
Santa Fe, NM
800-925-9387
*www.highcountrygardens.com*

**Julie Siegel**
Evanston, IL
847-733-9854
*www.jsiegeldesigns.com*

**Scott Spencer**
Fallbrook, CA
*js.spencer@sbcglobal.net*

**Jack Staub**
Hortulus Farm
Wrightstown, PA
215-598-0550
*www.hortulusfarm.com*

**Nan Sterman**
Plant Soup
Encinitas, CA
760-634-2902
*Info@PlantSoup.Com*

**Freeland and Sabrina
Tanner**
Proscape Landscape
Yountville, CA
707-226-2540

**Marcia Tatroe**
Aurora, CO
303-699-8958

**Brandon A. Tyson**
Brandon A. Tyson Landscape
Design
Napa, CA
707-290-2220

**Laurel Voran**
Chanticleer: A Pleasure
Garden
Wayne, PA
610-688-2919
*www.chanticleergarden.org*

**Nancy Webber**
Ground Xero
Austin, TX
512-657-2302

**Lenny Wilson**
Delaware Center for
Horticulture
Wilmington, DE
302-658-6262
*www.dehort.org*

**Jonathan Wright**
Chanticleer: A Pleasure
Garden
Wayne, PA
610-688-2919
*www.chanticleergarden.org*

# PLANT RESOURCES

If you can't find plants to make the best garden in your region from the vendors listed below, you need professional help (and I don't mean horticultural help). The nurseries that are listed as "wholesale only" are in this list because they offer valuable resources for planning gardens and finding plants.

Annie's Annuals & Perennials
Richmond, CA
888-266-4370
www.anniesannuals.com

The Antique Rose Emporium
Brenham, TX
800-441-0002
www.antiqueroseemporium.com

Bluebird Nursery
Clarkson, NE
800-356-9164
www.bluebirdnursery.com

Brent and Becky's Bulbs
Gloucester, VA
804-693-3966
www.brentandbeckysbulbs.com

Cactus Pruner
Lakewood, CO
303-232-8788
www.cactuspruner.com

Cistus Nursery
Sauvie Island, OR
503-621-2233
www.cistus.com

Digging Dog Nursery
Albion, CA
707-937-1130
www.diggingdog.com

High Country Gardens
Santa Fe, NM
800-925-9387
www.highcountrygardens.com

Monrovia (Wholesale Only)
www.monrovia.com

Mountain States Wholesale Nursery (Wholesale Only)
Litchfield Park, AZ
623-247-8509
www.mswn.com

Native Sons (Wholesale Only)
Arroyo Grande, CA
805-481-5996
www.nativeson.com

North Creek Nurseries (Wholesale Only)
Landenberg, PA
877-326-7584
www.northcreeknurseries.com

Prairie Nursery
Westfield, WI
800-476-9453
www.prairienursery.com

Plant Delights Nursery
Raleigh, NC
919-772-4794
www.plantdelights.com

Plant Select
http://129.82.181.23/

San Marcos Growers (Wholesale Only)
Santa Barbara, CA
805-683-1561
www.smgrowers.com

Seaside Gardens
Carpenteria, CA
805-684-6001
www.seaside-gardens.com

Siskiyou Rare Plant Nursery
Talent, OR
541-535-7103
www.srpn.net

Starr Nursery
Tucson, AZ
520-743-7052
www.starr-nursery.com

Sunny Border
Kensington, CT
www.sunnyborder.com

Timberline Gardens
Arvada, CO
303-420-4060
www.timberlinegardens.com

Yucca Do Nursery
Hempstead, TX
979-826-4580
www.yuccado.com

North American Rock Garden Society
Millwood, NY
www.nargs.org

Proven Winners
Sycamore, IL
877-865-5818
www.provenwinners.com

Small Plants
Horse Shoe, NC
www.smallplants.com

# PUBLIC GARDENS FOR DESIGN INSPIRATION

Several of the photos in this book feature the work of the brilliant horticulturists at the public gardens listed below. Visit these gardens for pleasure and further enlightenment.

Battery Park
New York, New York
*www.thebattery.org/gardens*

Chanticleer: A Pleasure
Garden
Wayne, PA
610-688-2919
*www.chanticleergarden.org*

Chicago Botanic Gardens
Glencoe, IL
847-835-5440
*www.chicagobotanic.org*

Kendrick Lake Park
Water-wise Garden
9351 West Jewell Avenue
Lakewood, Colorado

Longwood Gardens
Kennett Square, PA
610-388-1000
*www.longwoodgardens.org*

Denver Botanic Gardens
Denver, CO
720-865-3585
*www.botanicgardens.org*

Desert Botanical Garden
Phoenix, AZ
480-941-1225
*www.desertbotanical.org*

Lurie Garden
(Millennium Park)
Chicago, IL
312-742-1168
*www.millenniumpark.org/luriegarden*

The New York Botanical
Garden
Bronx, NY
718-817-8700
*www.nybg.org*

Olbrich Botanical Gardens
Madison, WI
608-246-4550
*www.olbrich.org*

Quail Botanical Gardens
Encinitas, CA
760-436-3036
*www.qbgardens.org*

Rancho Santa Ana Botanic
Garden
Claremont, CA
909-625-8767
*www.rsabg.org*

Tohono Chul Park
Tucson, AZ
520-742-6455
*www.tohonochulpark.org*

Wave Hill
Bronx, NY
718-549-3200
*www.wavehill.org*

# USDA HARDINESS ZONE MAP

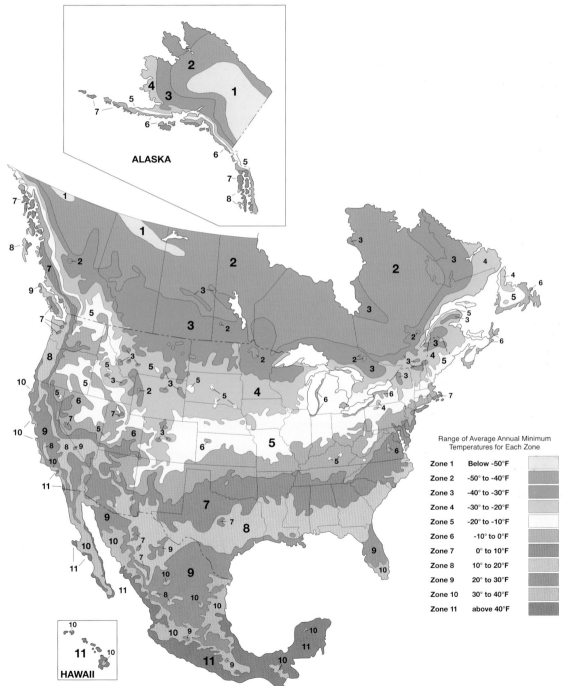

Range of Average Annual Minimum
Temperatures for Each Zone

| Zone 1 | Below -50°F |
| Zone 2 | -50° to -40°F |
| Zone 3 | -40° to -30°F |
| Zone 4 | -30° to -20°F |
| Zone 5 | -20° to -10°F |
| Zone 6 | -10° to 0°F |
| Zone 7 | 0° to 10°F |
| Zone 8 | 10° to 20°F |
| Zone 9 | 20° to 30°F |
| Zone 10 | 30° to 40°F |
| Zone 11 | above 40°F |

ALASKA

HAWAII

Designer Plant Combinations

# INDEX

Page references in **bold** indicate main entries; page references in *italics* indicate photos.

Designer Plant Combinations

glochids, removal of, 140
*phaeacantha* (sprawling prickly pear), **140**, *141*, *196*, **197**
Oriental poppy. *See Papaver*
*Origanum* × 'Rotkugel' (ornamental oregano), **44**, *45*
ornamental chives. *See Allium*
ornamental grasses, 127. *See also* grasses
ornamental onion, 15. *See Allium*
ornamental oregano. *See Origanum*
Oudolf, Piet, 8, 60, 64, 70, 100, 101, 178, 179, 194, 195, 198
overwintering plants, 111, 123
*Oxypetalum caeruleum* 'Heavenly Blue' (southern star), **156**, *157*

## P

*Panicum virgatum* (switchgrass), *104*, **105**
　'Dallas Blues', *88*, **89**
　'Heavy Metal', 64
　'Northwind', *116*, **117**
*Papaver* (poppy)
　× *rhoeas* (Shirley poppy), *108*, **109**
　*orientale* 'Türkenlouis' (oriental poppy), *130*, **131**
*Parkinsonia florida* (blue palo verde), **164**, *165*
*Parthenium integrifolium* (wild quinine), *96*, **97**
*Patrinia scabiosifolia*, *70*, **71**
Peace, Tom, 86
*Pelargonium* (geranium)
　*ionidiflorum* 'Pink Fairy Castles', **148**, *149*
　*sidoides*, *210*, **211**
*Pennisetum* (fountain grass)
　*alopecuroides* 'Little Bunny', *102*, **103**
　*setaceum* 'Rubrum' (purple fountain grass), *126*, **127**
*Penstemon*, 21
　*baccharifolius* (rock penstemon), *150*, **151**
　*barbatus,108*, **109**
　　'Elfin Pink' *48*, **49**
　*digitalis* 'Husker Red', *5*, **6**
　*pinifolius* (pineleaf penstemon), **48**, *49*

*pseudospectabilis* (Canyon penstemon), *46*, **47**
　*superbus*, 22, **23**
peonies, 198, *199*
perennials, 12–63. *See also* specific plant
*Perovskia atriplicifolia* (Russian sage), **8**, *9*, *50–51*, 51, **98**, *99*, *218*, *219*
　'Blue Spire', *62*, **63**
　'Little Spire', *76*, **77**, *112*, **113**, 113
*Persicaria*
　*amplexicaulis* ('Firetail' knotweed), **36**, *37*
　*polymorpha* (white dragon knotweed), *54*, **55**
　*virginiana* 'Lance Corporal' (fleeceflower), **178**, *179*
Phillips, Judith, 35, 52, 160
*Phlomis fruticosa* (Jerusalem sage), 179
*Phlox paniculata* (garden phlox), *50–51*, 51
*Physocarpus opulifolius* 'Seward' (Summer Wine), 135, 189
pincushion plant. *See Knautia macedonia*
pine. *See Pinus*
*Pinus mugo* var. *mugo* (dwarf mugo pine), *188*, **189**
*Planting Design* (Oudolf and Kingsbury), 8
plant resources, 229
Plant Select program, 8, 26
*Platycodon grandiflorus* (balloon flower), *174*, **175**, *226*, **227**
*Plectranthus*
　*argentatus* (silver spurflower), *222*, **223**
　*forsteri* 'Marginatus' (variegated plectranthus), **184**, *185*
　propagation of, 184
plumbago. *See Ceratostigma plumbaginoides*
*Polygonatum odoratum* 'Variegatum' (variegated Solomon's seal), *84*, **85**
ponytail grass. *See Nassella tenuissima*
poppy. *See Eschscholzia californica; Glaucium flavum; Hunnemannia fumarifolia; Papaver*
poppy mallow, 193

*Portulaca grandiflora* 'Yubi Red' and 'Yubi Yellow' (rose moss), *180*, *181*
prairie coneflower. *See Echinacea*
prairie dock. *See Silphium*
prairie garden, 56, 60, 96–97
prairie zinnia. *See Zinnia*
prickly pear. *See Opuntia*
primrose. *See Oenothera*
prostrate rosemary. *See Rosmarinus officinalis*
Proven Winners, 40
pruning, 160, 204
*Prunus*
　× *cistena* (purple-leaved sand cherry), *226*, **227**
　*persica* 'Bonfire' (dwarf peach), *206*, **207**
public gardens, 230. *See also* specific garden
purple coneflower. *See Echinacea*
purple heart. *See Tradescantia*
purple lance astilbe. *See Astilbe chinensis*
purple-leaved sand cherry. *See Prunus*
purple love grass. *See Eragrostis spectabilis*
purple moor grass. *See Molinia caerulea*

## Q

Queen Anne's lace. *See Daucus carota*
queen of the meadows. *See Filipendula ulmaria*

## R

*Ratibida pinnata* (gray coneflower), 60
rattlesnake master. *See Eryngium yuccifolium*
redbud. *See Cercis canadensis*
red-hot poker. *See Kniphofia*
repeated shapes, 144, 183
reseeding, 22
*Robinia pseudoacacia* 'Frisia' (golden locust), *74*, **75**, *210*, **211**
rock cress. *See Aubrieta*
rockery, 139, 148, 184
rock rose. *See Helianthemum nummularium*

# Other Storey Titles You Will Enjoy

**Covering Ground,** by Barbara W. Ellis.
Creative ideas to landscape with hardworking and attractive ground covers.
224 pages. Paper. ISBN 978-1-58017-665-1.

**Fallscaping,** by Nancy J. Ondra and Stephanie Cohen.
A comprehensive guide to the best plants for brightening late-season landscapes.
240 pages. Paper with flaps. ISBN 978-1-58017-680-4.
Hardcover with jacket. ISBN 978-1-58017-681-1.

**Foliage,** by Nancy J. Ondra.
A eye-opening garden guide to the brilliant colors and textures of dozens
of plants, all chosen for the unique appeal of their leaves.
304 pages. Paper with flaps. ISBN 978-1-58017-648-4.
Hardcover with jacket. ISBN 978-1-58017-654-5.

**Grasses,** by Nancy J. Ondra.
Photographs and plans for 20 gardens that highlight the beauty of grasses
in combination with perennials, annuals, and shrubs.
144 pages. Paper with flaps. ISBN 978-1-58017-423-7.

**Hardy Succulents,** by Gwen Moore Kelaidis.
A complete resource to bring a touch of the unexpected from the Southwest
— from agaves to ice plants and from sedums to sempervivums.
160 pages. Paper with flaps. ISBN 978-1-58017-700-9.
Hardcover. ISBN 978-1-58017-701-6.

**The Perennial Gardener's Design Primer,** by Stephanie Cohen and Nancy J. Ondra.
A lively, authoritative guide to creating perennial gardens using basic design
principles for putting plants together in pleasing and practical ways.
320 pages. Paper. ISBN 978-1-58017-543-2.
Hardcover with jacket. ISBN 978-1-58017-545-6.

These and other books from Storey Publishing are available
wherever quality books are sold or by calling 1-800-441-5700.
Visit us at *www.storey.com*.